Stephen Donald

Stage 4 Mathematics

A development through activity

Textbook

HEINEMANN
EDUCATIONAL

Stage 4   Contents

Stage 4 Contents

Part 1 Acknowledgements

p2. David Redfern
pp5&6. Richard Jones, Guinness Book
          of Records, The Post Office
p9. Trusthouse Forte
p10. Britain on View
p24. Oxprint
p28. Allsport

Thousands

1 Make digit cards like these.
Use them for the questions below.

2 Use the digit cards. Make, and then write, **four** numbers which are each
  (a) greater than 9 but less than 100, e.g. 53,
  (b) greater than 99 but less than 1000, e.g. 532,
  (c) greater than 999 but less than 9000, e.g. 5328.

3 Make, and then write, an **even** number which has
  (a) 2 digits,   (b) 3 digits,   (c) 4 digits.

4 Use all four cards. Make, and then write,
  (a) the largest possible number,   (b) the smallest possible number.

5 Lay out the cards for each number shown. Write the numbers.

(a)
thousands	hundreds	tens	units
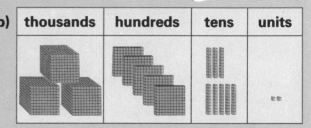

(b)
thousands	hundreds	tens	units

(c)
thousands	hundreds	tens	units
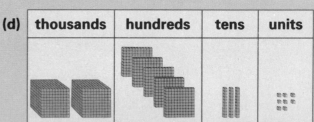

(d)
thousands	hundreds	tens	units

6 Lay out the cards for each number. Write the number:
  (a) three thousand eight hundred and fifty-two,
  (b) eight thousand two hundred and thirty-five,
  (c) two thousand three hundred and fifty-eight,
  (d) five thousand eight hundred and twenty-three.

7265 is seven thousand two hundred and sixty-five.

7 Write in words: (a) 4617   (b) 9170   (c) 6904   (d) 8023   (e) 9009

8 Do this ⟶
for these numbers:
  (a) 7439
  (b) 6708

4126 is **4** thousands **1** hundred **2** tens and **6** units
or   **41** hundreds **2** tens and **6** units
or   **412** tens and **6** units
or   **4126** units

9 You may use a calculator to find:
  (a) 4216 + 1378 + 2542   (b) 7165 − 5108   (c) 2048 + 217 + 79
  (d) 407 + 82 + 8314   (e) 6 + 3120 + 835   (f) 6376 + 793 − 88

Ask your teacher if you can play 'Say the number'.

Lots of thousands

We write	**five** thousand	or	**5** thousand	as	**5000**
	twelve thousand	or	**12** thousand	as	**12 000**
	one hundred and sixty thousand	or	**160** thousand	as	**160 000**

1 Write these numbers:
  (a) six thousand,   **(b)** 15 thousand,   **(c)** twenty thousand,
  (d) forty-two thousand,   **(e)** one hundred thousand,   **(f)** 123 thousand.

2 Write these using the word **thousand**:
  (a) 18 000   **(b)** 60 000   **(c)** 89 000   **(d)** 103 000   **(e)** 140 000   **(f)** 213 000

3 Write the number which is **one thousand more** than:
  (a) 16 000,   **(b)** fifty thousand,   **(c)** 29 thousand,
  (d) one hundred and fourteen thousand.

4 Write the number which is **1000 less** than:
  (a) eighty-two thousand,   **(b)** 14 thousand,   **(c)** forty thousand,   **(d)** 210 thousand.

One hundred and twenty-six thousand nine hundred and forty tickets were sold for the Pop Concert.

126 940

5 Write each number:
  (a) The official attendance at today's match was seventy-four thousand six hundred and twenty-four.
  (b) The population of this town is one hundred and ten thousand four hundred and seventy.
  (c) Four hundred and sixty-six thousand and forty have visited this exhibition.
  (d) Six hundred and thirty-eight thousand seven hundred and two people voted.
  (e) Three hundred and twenty thousand six hundred and ninety papers were sold today.
  (f) We take eight hundred thousand to work every day.

6 Write each number **in words**:
  (a) At today's match   **17 698**   **(b)** At Thursday's match   **21 735**
  (c) At the semi-final   **49 320**   **(d)** Watching the final   **231 400**

Millions

One thousand thousand or **1000** thousand is called **one million.**

We write one million as   **1 000 000**

seventeen million as   **17 000 000**

1   Write these numbers:
   (a) three million,   **(b)** 6 million,   **(c)** ten million,   **(d)** 25 million,   **(e)** thirty million.

2   Write these using the word **million:**
   (a) 5 000 000   **(b)** 9 000 000   **(c)** 14 000 000   **(d)** 52 000 000   **(e)** 69 000 000

Half a million is $\frac{1}{2}$ of 1000 thousand,
which is 500 thousand or **500 000.**

3   Write these numbers:
   (a) six and a half million,   **(b)** $8\frac{1}{2}$ million,   **(c)** twelve and a half million,   **(d)** $19\frac{1}{2}$ million.

(e)    **(f)**    **(g)**

4   Write these numbers in another way:

(a)    **(b)**    **(c)**

5   Write, in figures, the number which is $\frac{1}{2}$ million less than:
   (a) 6 million,   **(b)** $4\frac{1}{2}$ million,   **(c)** 10 million,   **(d)** 800 000.

6   Write, in figures, the number which is 200 thousand more than:
   (a) 1 million,   **(b)** 6 500 000,   **(c)** 800 000,   **(d)** $2\frac{1}{2}$ million.

6 in the number 1 5**6**2 143 is 60 **thousands.**
6 in the number **6** 432 185 is   6 **millions.**

7   What is the value of the **4** in each of these numbers:
   (a) 1 2**4**9 319   **(b)** **4** 375 610   **(c)** 8**4**0 123   **(d)** 5 **4**22 912   **(e)** **4**3 167 392?

8   What is the value of the **red** digit in each of these numbers:
   (a) 1 **2**34 567   **(b)** 2 4**2**5 681   **(c)** 5**3**4 015   **(d)** 1 929 0**0**0   **(e)** 10 5**0**0 000?

About how many?

Each full packet contains 10 sweets.

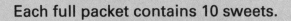

There are between 30 and 40 sweets.

There are between 30 and 40 sweets.

There are **30 sweets** to the nearest ten.

There are **40 sweets** to the nearest ten.

1 Write the number of sweets **to the nearest ten:**

(a) 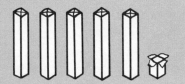 (b)  (c)

2 Do Workbook Page 1.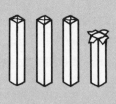

3 Write each of these numbers **to the nearest ten:**
  (a) 43   (b) 77   (c) 256   (d) 184   (e) 368   (f) 302   (g) 199
  (h) 5927 (i) 1843 (j) 998   (k) 1219 (l) 1587 (m) 2006 (n) 7991

Each jar holds 100 marbles when full.

There are between 200 and 300 marbles. There are about **200 marbles to the nearest hundred.**

There are between 100 and 200 marbles. There are about **200 marbles to the nearest hundred.**

4 Write the number of marbles **to the nearest hundred:**
(a)    (b)

5 Do Workbook Page 2.

6 Write each of these numbers **to the nearest hundred:**
  (a) 460   (b) 920   (c) 1435 (d) 8749 (e) 13 210 (f) 4555 (g) 29 860
  (h) 2046 (i) 32 088 (j) 59 111 (k) 3990 (l) 16 970 (m) 1999 (n) 8985

Ask your teacher if you should do Workbook Page 3.

Thousands and millions

**Use the opposite page to find the answers to the following questions.
You may use a calculator to help you.**

1 Write, in figures, the number of
   (a) Richard Jones' rubber bands,   **(b)** letters delivered daily by the Post Office,
   (c) people called Chang in China,   **(d)** kilometres walked by Johann Hurlinger.

2 For each of these, which is more and by how many:
   (a) the number of people called Smith in Great Britain **or**
      the number of Changs in China,
   (b) the number of letters **or** the number of parcels delivered daily,
   (c) the number of kilometres walked forward by David Kunst
      or the number of kilometres walked backwards by Pennie Wingo?

3 How many dominoes were actually toppled by
   (a) Michael Cairney at his first attempt,
   (b) Bob Speca when he attempted a hundred thousand?

4 Copy and complete this table ⟶ about toppling the dominoes.

Record holder	Dominoes toppled	Better than the old record by
Bob	22 222	
Michael	33 266	11 044
Bob	50 000	
Bob		
Michael		

5 Find the **total** number of
   (a) kilometres walked by all three men,
   (b) parcels and letters delivered each day by the Post Office,
   (c) dominoes toppled by Bob in his three attempts,
   (d) dominoes toppled by Michael in his two attempts,
   (e) dominoes toppled by both Bob and Michael.

6 Write each of these **to the nearest thousand:**
   (a) the number of different addresses receiving mail each day,
   (b) the number of kilometres walked by David Kunst,
   (c) the number of kilometres walked by Pennie Wingo,
   (d) the number of dominoes toppled in Michael's last record attempt.

7 Make up and write a record breaking story of your own using large numbers.

Ask your teacher what to do next.

Record Breakers

14 year old Richard Jones of Hemel Hempstead made a ball with 67 thousand rubber bands – a record breaking ball.

What's in a Name

There are eight hundred thousand people in Great Britain with the name of SMITH.

The commonest surname in China is CHANG. Seventy-five million people have this name.

Walkers

David Kunst of Minnesota walked 27 360 kilometres 'around the world'. Pennie Wingo of Texas covered 12 875 kilometres walking backwards! Johann Hurlinger of Austria walked 14 hundred kilometres on his hands.

The Daily Mail

The Post Office delivers $32\frac{1}{2}$ million letters and 600 thousand parcels each day to a total of 22 million different addresses in Great Britain.

Domino Toppling

Bob Speca in Pennsylvania set a record by toppling 22 222 dominoes. Michael Cairney in Leeds decided to do better and attempted 33 333, but 67 did not fall. However, the record was his. Bob Speca's answer to this challenge was to topple 50 000. He then attempted 100 000 but 2500 did not fall. Michael had one more try. He spent 13 days setting out the dominoes and then in one hour 169 713 toppled.

Multiplying by 2, 3, 4, 5, 10

1 Find:
(a) 2×5 (b) 3×4 (c) 4×9 (d) 5×5 (e) 3×6 (f) 4×8 (g) 10×6

2 (a) $(3 \times 7) + 6$ (b) $(4 \times 7) - 3$ (c) $20 + (2 \times 9)$ (d) $30 - (10 \times 2)$

(e) $(10 \times 3) + (3 \times 8)$ (f) $(10 \times 6) - (4 \times 5)$ (g) $(10 \times 8) - (5 \times 8)$
(h) $(10 \times 10) - (5 \times 2)$

3
(a) 32×3
(b) 17×5
(c) 70×4
(d) 78×2
(e) 104×2
(f) 200×5

(g) 419×5
(h) 983×3
(i) 265×4
(j) 2186×2
(k) 1809×4
(l) 2597×3

To multiply by ten, move the digits **one** place to the left.

$$356 \times 10 = 3560$$

---

4 (a) 10×47 (b) 10×371 (c) 205×10 (d) 10×890 (e) 700×10

5 Which is greater **10×403** or **4×1007**?

6 Write a word problem for the multiplication 3×365.

You may use a calculator.

7 Four people each received £7852 for a
win on the football pools.
What was the total money won?

8 Here are the winnings from football pools.
Calculate the total won in each case.

(a)
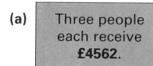
Three people each receive **£4562**.

(b)
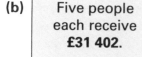
Five people each receive **£31 402**.

(c)
Eight people each receive **£27 150**.

Multiplying by 6, 7, 8, 9

1 **(a)** Use squared paper to make **two** answer squares like this ⟶

    (b) Write the answers to **X** and **Y** in your answer squares.

X

6×8	6×6	7×9
6×3	7×7	6×5
6×9	7×5	7×6

Y

8×7	9×9	8×6
8×9	8×8	8×10
9×5	9×7	9×6

(c) For square **X**, colour blue all products less than 40.

(d) For square **Y**, colour red all products greater than 60.

2 **(a)** $(6 \times 5) + 4$ **(b)** $(7 \times 8) - 6$ **(c)** $(6 \times 9) - 6$ **(d)** $(7 \times 6) + 9$

    (e) $(8 \times 6) + 3$ **(f)** $(9 \times 4) - 4$ **(g)** $(8 \times 5) - 8$ **(h)** $(9 \times 8) + 8$

3 Multiply each number by 6:   **(a)** 84   **(b)** 139   **(c)** 405

4 Multiply each number by 7:   **(d)** 360   **(e)** 872   **(f)** 1028

5 **(a)**   26
     ×9

    (b)   43
        ×8

    (c) 500
        ×9

    (d) 205
        ×8

    (e) 348
        ×8

    (f) 999
        ×9

    (g) 826
        ×8

    (h) 478
        ×9

    (i) 750
        ×8

    (j) 567
        ×9

    (k) 1218
        ×8

    (l) 1023
        ×9

You may use a calculator.

6 Each car costs £5795. Find the total cost of   **(a)** the 6 blue cars,   **(b)** the 9 red cars.

7 The weight of each car is 1128 kg. Find the total weight of   **(a)** the blue cars,
    (b) **all** the cars.

8 At Scott's garage, 2 blue cars are delivered. At Peter's garage 5 red cars are delivered. How much more does Peter pay than Scott?

9 What is the total cost of the cars left on the transporters?

Ask your teacher if you should do Workbook Pages 5 and 6.

W

Grand hotel

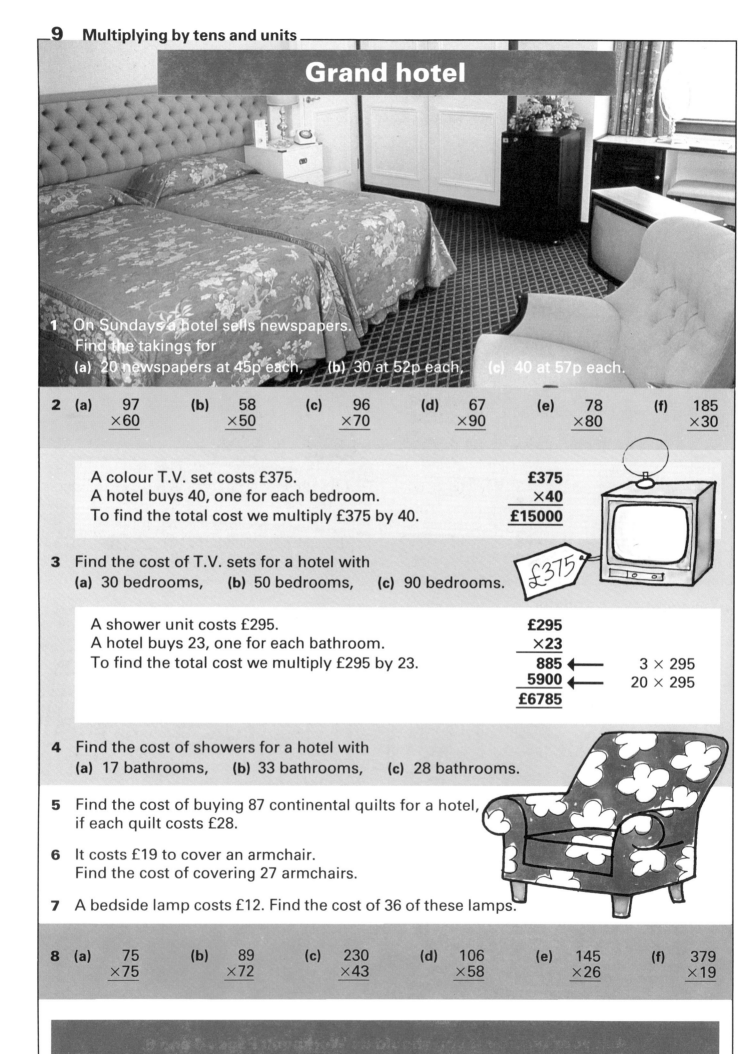

1   On Sundays a hotel sells newspapers.
    Find the takings for
    (a) 20 newspapers at 45p each,   (b) 30 at 52p each,   (c) 40 at 57p each.

2 (a)   97   (b)   58   (c)   96   (d)   67   (e)   78   (f)   185
      ×60   ×50   ×70   ×90   ×80   ×30

A colour T.V. set costs £375.   £375
A hotel buys 40, one for each bedroom.   ×40
To find the total cost we multiply £375 by 40.   £15000

3   Find the cost of T.V. sets for a hotel with
    (a) 30 bedrooms,   (b) 50 bedrooms,   (c) 90 bedrooms.

A shower unit costs £295.   £295
A hotel buys 23, one for each bathroom.   ×23
To find the total cost we multiply £295 by 23.   885 ←—— 3 × 295
                                                        5900 ←—— 20 × 295
                                                        £6785

4   Find the cost of showers for a hotel with
    (a) 17 bathrooms,   (b) 33 bathrooms,   (c) 28 bathrooms.

5   Find the cost of buying 87 continental quilts for a hotel,
    if each quilt costs £28.

6   It costs £19 to cover an armchair.
    Find the cost of covering 27 armchairs.

7   A bedside lamp costs £12. Find the cost of 36 of these lamps.

8 (a)   75   (b)   89   (c)   230   (d)   106   (e)   145   (f)   379
      ×75   ×72   ×43   ×58   ×26   ×19

Caravans and cars

Mr Black owns 29 caravans.
The cost of hiring a caravan
is shown below.

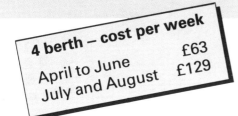

4 berth – cost per week
April to June £63
July and August £129

1 One week in April he hired out
15 caravans.
One week in July he hired
out 29 caravans.
Find the difference in his earnings
for these weeks.

2 At the end of the season he sold
4 caravans for £285 each.
How much did he get from the sale?

3 The next season he charged the same amounts for the hire of his
remaining caravans. Find:
(a) the highest income he could **now** expect for one week in April,
(b) the highest income for one week in July,
(c) the difference in income between these two weeks.

4 Find the product of (a) 86 and 97, (b) 135 and 59, (c) 342 and 18.

You may use a calculator.

5 A company bought 24 new cars
each costing £6235 for its salesmen.
What was the total cost?

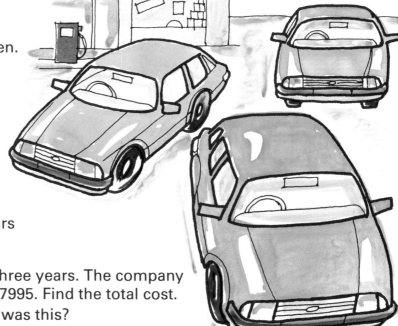

6 A salesman drives an average of
2500 miles (4000 km) per month.
How far will he travel in one year
(a) in miles, (b) in km?

7 Another salesman averages
2850 miles (4560 km) per month.
How far will he travel in three years
(a) in miles, (b) in km?

8 (a) The cars were replaced after three years. The company
bought 28 cars each costing £7995. Find the total cost.
(b) How much less than £250 000 was this?

Multiplying by 100 and 1000

1 Find:
(a) 576 × 10   (b) 2376 × 10   (c) 10 × 8900   (d) 10 × 4005   (e) 10 000 × 10

576 multiplied by 100

576 × 100 = 576 × 10 × 10
= (576 × 10) × 10
= 5760 × 10
= 57 600

576 × 100 = 57 600

To multiply by 100, move the digits **two** places to the left.

2 Use the short method to multiply each of these numbers by 100:
(a) 542   (b) 837   (c) 5072   (d) 1900   (e) 9006   (f) 8000

3 Pop Van Twinkle slept for a hundred years. How many months was this?

4 A box contains 200 pencils. How many pencils will a hundred boxes hold?

576 multiplied by 1000

576 × 1000 = 576 × 100 × 10
= (576 × 100) × 10
= 57 600 × 10
= 576 000

576 × 1000 = 576 000

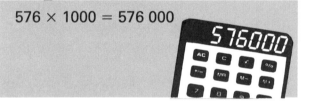

To multiply by 1000, move the digits **three** places to the left.

5 Multiply each of these numbers by 1000:
(a) 28   (b) 712   (c) 560   (d) 308   (e) 8006   (f) 5000

6 (a) A club has one thousand members. Each member was asked to give £5 for repairs to the club house. How much money is this altogether?

(b) One hundred of the members did **not** give £5. How much money was collected?

(c) The thousand members were then each given 20 tickets to sell in a raffle. How many tickets was this altogether?

(d) Each ticket cost 10p. How much money could the raffle raise?

7 (a) 100 × 471   (b) 3620 × 1000   (c) 20 505 × 100   (d) 1000 × 700

Investigations

1 **(a)** Copy this number square on squared paper.

25	15	9	8	56
40	29	54	12	35
16	14	23	7	49
63	35	17	28	20
9	24	18	45	25

(c) Find and draw another path.
Do not move diagonally.

(b) The red line shows a path through the number square. Each number on the path is in the same multiplication table as the next number.

start

25	15	9	8	56
40	29	54	12	35
16	14	23	7	49
63	35	17	28	20
9	24	18	45	25

finish

25 and **40** are both stations of the five times table.

40 and **16** are both stations of the eight times table . . . . and so on.

2 Find a path for this number square. This time you may find 'dead ends' before you discover the correct path.

25	35	42	12	10
18	32	49	36	63
35	20	90	54	40
81	8	43	7	16
21	64	24	15	25

3 **(a)** Write the number sequence 17, 16, 15, 14, 13, 12 as shown ⟶

$$\begin{array}{ccc} 17 & 16 & 15 \\ \times 12 & \times 13 & \times 14 \\ \hline \end{array}$$

(b) Use a calculator to do the multiplications.

4 Repeat this for sequences of six numbers starting with **(a)** 29, **(b)** 65.
What do you notice about your answers in each case?

5 Copy and try to complete these without multiplying or using a calculator.
Check your answers.

(a)
$$\begin{array}{ccc} 39 & 38 & 37 \\ \times 34 & \times 35 & \times 36 \\ \hline & & 1332 \\ \hline \end{array}$$

(b)
$$\begin{array}{ccc} 75 & 74 & 73 \\ \times 70 & \times 71 & \times 72 \\ \hline 5250 & & \\ \hline \end{array}$$

6 Investigate what happens when you use a similar sequence of **eight** numbers.

7 Use the pattern of your results to complete this sequence.
Check your answers with a calculator.

$$\begin{array}{ccccc} 104 & 103 & 102 & 101 & 100 \\ \times 95 & \times 96 & \times 97 & \times 98 & \times 99 \\ \hline & & & & 9900 \\ \hline \end{array}$$

Ask your teacher if you should do Puzzle Cards 1, 3, 5, 7, 9 and Calculator Cards 11, 13, 15, 17, 19

Adding

Adding tens first

Do these mentally and write your answers:

1 (a) 25 + 40   (b) 79 + 10   (c) 14 + 70   (d) 18 + 80   (e) 52 + 30
      (f) 37 + 60   (g) 23 + 50   (h) 77 + 20   (i) 41 + 40   (j) 26 + 50

2 (a) 49 + 2   (b) 33 + 9   (c) 56 + 4   (d) 45 + 8   (e) 84 + 8
      (f) 37 + 7   (g) 78 + 3   (h) 42 + 7   (i) 77 + 6   (j) 68 + 5

> To find 34 + 57, start with 34,
>
> **add 50**   to give 84 then   **add 7**   to give 91.
>
> We can write: **34 + 57 ⟶ 84 + 7 ⟶ 91**

3 Do these in the same way:
      (a) 62 + 24   (b) 53 + 38   (c) 27 + 45   (d) 61 + 27   (e) 38 + 48

4 Do these mentally and write your answers:
      (a) 25 + 33   (b) 35 + 46   (c) 64 + 29   (d) 41 + 45   (e) 23 + 67
      (f) 32 + 57   (g) 54 + 28   (h) 46 + 22   (i) 71 + 18   (j) 43 + 49

Another method of adding

| 29 is 30 − 1 | | 48 is 50 − 2 | | 67 is 70 − 3 |

5 Write these in the same way:
      (a) 39   (b) 88   (c) 59   (d) 17   (e) 68   (f) 47

> This method works best for adding when one of the
> numbers has a units digit of 7, 8 or 9.
>
> To find 46 + 28, start with 46,
>
> **add 30**   to give 76 then   **subtract 2**   to give 74.
>
> We can write: **46 + 28 ⟶ 76 − 2 ⟶ 74**

6 Do these in the same way:
      (a) 38 + 39   (b) 36 + 27   (c) 34 + 48   (d) 25 + 59   (e) 42 + 38

7 Do these mentally and write your answers:
      (a) 34 + 57   (b) 39 + 39   (c) 36 + 29   (d) 47 + 37   (e) 19 + 58
      (f) 42 + 29   (g) 35 + 48   (h) 41 + 47   (i) 23 + 69   (j) 37 + 28

8 Use **either of the above methods** to do these mentally. Write your answers.
      (a) 26 + 26   (b) 43 + 35   (c) 33 + 49   (d) 65 + 18   (e) 43 + 34
      (f) 29 + 46   (g) 37 + 24   (h) 62 + 27   (i) 73 + 26   (j) 39 + 52

Subtracting

Subtracting tens first

Do these mentally and write your answers:

1 (a) 43 − 10   (b) 68 − 40   (c) 77 − 60   (d) 65 − 20   (e) 81 − 50
   (f) 98 − 60   (g) 52 − 20   (h) 94 − 70   (i) 99 − 30   (j) 76 − 40

2 (a) 47 − 8   (b) 63 − 6   (c) 88 − 4   (d) 32 − 8   (e) 58 − 7
   (f) 54 − 5   (g) 75 − 9   (h) 23 − 7   (i) 67 − 3   (j) 85 − 9

> To find 87 − 33, start with 87, **subtract 30** to give 57, then **subtract 3** to give 54.
>
> We can write: **87 − 33 ⟶ 57 − 3 ⟶ 54**

3 Do these in the same way:
   (a) 68 − 45   (b) 73 − 26   (c) 45 − 17   (d) 89 − 34   (e) 57 − 28

4 Do these mentally and write your answers:
   (a) 49 − 26   (b) 98 − 54   (c) 57 − 33   (d) 66 − 32   (e) 75 − 21
   (f) 83 − 47   (g) 32 − 19   (h) 74 − 48   (i) 61 − 25   (j) 90 − 43

> To find 65 − 38,   **subtract 40** to give 25, then   **add 2** to give 27.
>
> We can write: **65 − 38 ⟶ 25 + 2 ⟶ 27**

5 Do these in the same way:
   (a) 92 − 49   (b) 65 − 37   (c) 73 − 28   (d) 46 − 19   (e) 84 − 48

6 Do these mentally and write your answers:
   (a) 60 − 39   (b) 54 − 29   (c) 84 − 38   (d) 72 − 57   (e) 91 − 69
   (f) 77 − 28   (g) 83 − 48   (h) 55 − 27   (i) 66 − 39   (j) 94 − 58

Adding equal amounts

To find
$$\begin{array}{r} 72 \\ -43 \\ \hline \end{array} \longrightarrow \boxed{\text{Add 7 to both numbers.}} \longrightarrow \begin{array}{r} 79 \\ -50 \\ \hline \end{array}$$

We can write:
$$\begin{array}{r} 72 \\ -43 \\ \hline \end{array} \longrightarrow \begin{array}{r} 79 \\ -50 \\ \hline 29 \end{array}$$

It is easier to subtract 50.

7 Do these in the same way:

(a) $\begin{array}{r} 31 \\ -19 \\ \hline \end{array}$ (b) $\begin{array}{r} 80 \\ -28 \\ \hline \end{array}$ (c) $\begin{array}{r} 73 \\ -35 \\ \hline \end{array}$ (d) $\begin{array}{r} 64 \\ -37 \\ \hline \end{array}$ (e) $\begin{array}{r} 95 \\ -46 \\ \hline \end{array}$ (f) $\begin{array}{r} 52 \\ -24 \\ \hline \end{array}$

(g) $\begin{array}{r} 86 \\ -68 \\ \hline \end{array}$ (h) $\begin{array}{r} 72 \\ -33 \\ \hline \end{array}$ (i) $\begin{array}{r} 41 \\ -27 \\ \hline \end{array}$ (j) $\begin{array}{r} 53 \\ -29 \\ \hline \end{array}$ (k) $\begin{array}{r} 62 \\ -26 \\ \hline \end{array}$ (l) $\begin{array}{r} 71 \\ -23 \\ \hline \end{array}$

Multiplying

Do these mentally and write your answers.

1 Multiply each number by 100:
   (a) 12   **(b)** 43   **(c)** 60   **(d)** 75
   (e) 123   **(f)** 81   **(g)** 96   **(h)** 100

2 Divide each of these numbers by 2:
   (a) 2400   **(b)** 5600   **(c)** 42 800   **(d)** 4700   **(e)** 3500   **(f)** 7000
   (g) 9900   **(h)** 6100   **(i)** 5300   **(j)** 3200   **(k)** 2800   **(l)** 13 500

Multiplying by 50

To find 37×50, start with 37,

          multiply by 100   to give 3700, then   **divide by 2**   to give 1850.

We can write: $37 \times 100 \longrightarrow 3700 \div 2 \longrightarrow 1850$

3 Do these in the same way:
   (a) 26×50 **(b)** 50×84 **(c)** 49×50 **(d)** 77×50 **(e)** 13×50

4 Do these mentally and write your answers:
   (a) 46×50 **(b)** 50×80 **(c)** 27×50 **(d)** 102×50 **(e)** 50×53 **(f)** 91×50

      1 ten $\times$ 1 ten   is 1 hundred $\longrightarrow$ 100
      2 tens $\times$ 4 tens is 8 hundreds $\longrightarrow$ 800

To find 60×70, 6 tens $\times$ 7 tens $\longrightarrow$ 42 hundreds

We can write: $60 \times 70 \longrightarrow 4200$

5 Do these mentally and write the answers:
   (a) 20×30 **(b)** 30×50 **(c)** 90×40 **(d)** 70×50 **(e)** 80×60

Approximate answers

43 is 40 to the nearest ten.   78 is 80 to the nearest ten.

To find 43×78:

We can write: 43×78 is about 40×80 43×78 is about **3200**

6 Find approximate answers for:
   (a) 43×86 **(b)** 27×52 **(c)** 46×99 **(d)** 33×31 **(e)** 29×38
   (f) 37×41 **(g)** 58×74 **(h)** 22×81 **(i)** 68×92 **(j)** 61×77

£7·99 and all that

We often see prices like these:

Each price is nearly a whole number of pounds. The skirt costs nearly £8.

1 Write the price, to the nearest pound, for each of the other items.

2 Find the approximate cost, in pounds, of
(a) a dress and a hat, (b) a skirt, a blouse, and a dress, (c) all four items,
(d) two blouses, (e) three dresses, (f) four hats.

3 The skirt costs £7·99 which is **£8 less 1p** Write the price of the other items in this way.

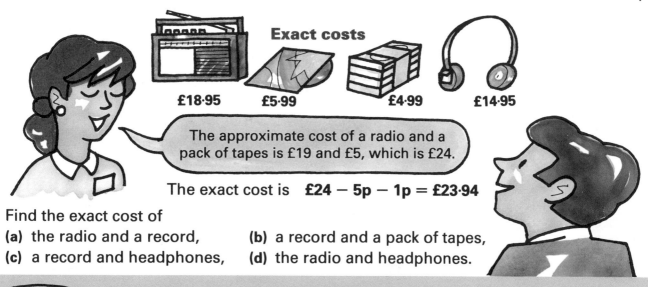

Exact costs

£18·95   £5·99   £4·99   £14·95

The approximate cost of a radio and a pack of tapes is £19 and £5, which is £24.

The exact cost is **£24 − 5p − 1p = £23·94**

4 Find the exact cost of
(a) the radio and a record, (b) a record and a pack of tapes,
(c) a record and headphones, (d) the radio and headphones.

Multiplying by 100

100 cans cost 45p × 100 ⟶ 4500p ⟶ £45.

When multiplying by 100, **pence become pounds.**

5 Write the cost of 100 of each of these:

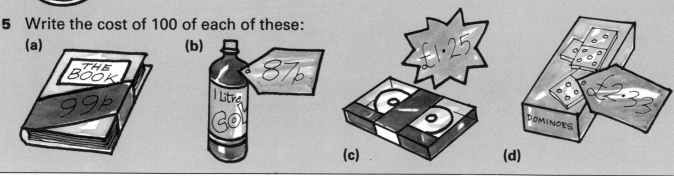

(a)   (b)   (c)   (d)

Ask your teacher what to do next.

Finding positions

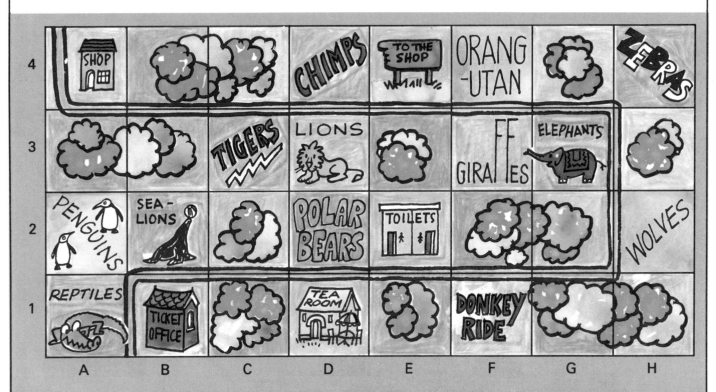

This is a plan of the zoo. The **columns** are marked A to H. The **rows** are marked 1 to 4. At position D1 there is the tea room. The zebras are at position H4.

1 What do you find at
    (a) C3,   **(b)** D4,   **(c)** F3,   **(d)** E4,   **(e)** D3,   **(f)** A2,   **(g)** E2,   **(h)** D2?

2 Where do you find the
    (a) shop,   **(b)** elephants,   **(c)** donkey ride,   **(d)** sea-lions,
    (e) orang-utan,   **(f)** wolves,   **(g)** ticket office,   **(h)** reptiles?

king   queen   bishop

castle   knight   pawn

3 On the chessboard there is a red pawn at F7.
At A1 there is a black bishop.
Name the pieces at positions
    (a) A4,   **(b)** E2,   **(c)** B3,   **(d)** H8.

4 Where is the
    (a) black knight,   **(b)** black queen,
    (c) red king,   **(d)** black castle,
    (e) red queen,   **(f)** red knight?

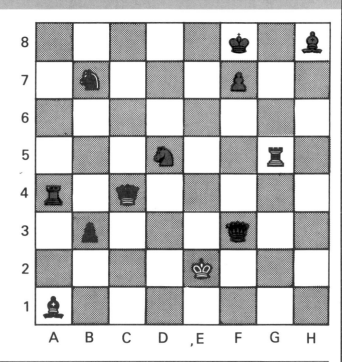

Do Workbook Page 7, questions 1 to 3.

W

Position by numbers

On this grid **both** columns **and** rows are numbered.
The position of the blue triangle is 2 along and 4 up.
We call this position (2,4).
At (6,1) there is a green square.

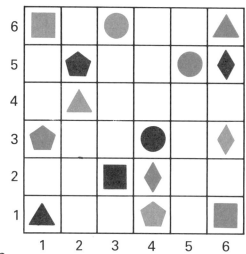

1 Name the colour and shape at these positions:
(a) (1,3), (b) (4,2), (c) (3,6), (d) (5,5),
(e) (6,6), (f) (2,5).

2 Give the positions of these shapes:
(a) red square, (b) red triangle,
(c) blue rhombus, (d) blue square,
(e) red circle, (f) red rhombus, (g) blue pentagon.

3 **Do Workbook Page 7, questions 5 and 6.**

4 This grid contains every letter except **Z**.

5	V	H	T	I	M
4	R	U	G	J	K
3	C	Q	W	L	X
2	S	B	O	P	N
1	Y	D	A	E	F
	1	2	3	4	5

A is at (3,1), **B** is at (2,2), and so on.
The code for the word **TEAM** is:

(3,5) (4,1) (3,1) (5,5)

T E A M

(a) Decode this message: (3,5) (2,5) (4,1)

(2,2)(4,1)(1,2)(3,5)   (4,2)(4,3)(3,1)(1,1)(4,1)(1,4)

(2,4)(1,2)(2,4)(3,1)(4,3)(4,3)(1,1)   (3,3)(4,5)(5,2)(1,2)

(b) Send a message to a friend in this code.

5 (a) Copy this grid on centimetre squared paper.
(b) Colour these squares red:

(1,6)(1,4)(2,5)(2,1)(3,3)(4,3)(5,5)(5,1)(6,6)(6,4)

(c) Colour these squares blue:

(3,6)(5,3)(2,4)(1,2)(5,4)(2,3)(4,6)(6,2)

(d) Draw the line of symmetry of
the coloured pattern.

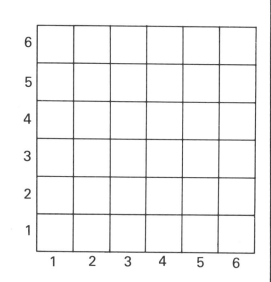

W

Co-ordinates

On this grid both sets of **lines** are marked 0 to 5.
A is the point of intersection of the line **3 along**
and the line **2 up**.
The point **A** has **co-ordinates (3,2)**.
The point **B** has **co-ordinates (0,4)**.

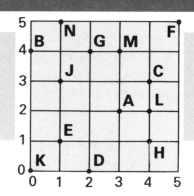

1 Write the co-ordinates of all the marked
points like this: **A** (3,2), **B** (0,4), and so on.

2 Look at this aerial view of a fishing fleet. What are the co-ordinates of
(a) Dolly, (b) Lady Jean, (c) Fearless, (d) Venture, (e) Sea-mew, (f) Puffin?

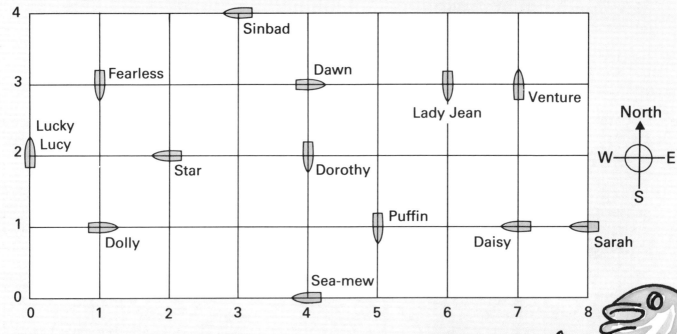

3 Which boats have co-ordinates
(a) (0,2), (b) (2,2), (c) (8,1), (d) (7,1), (e) (4,2), (f) (4,3)?

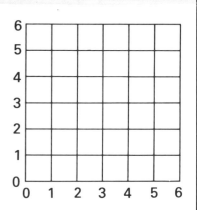

4 The grid lines are 1 kilometre apart.
What is the distance between (a) Dolly and Puffin, (b) Dawn and Sea-mew?

5 (a) How far West of Venture is Fearless?
(b) Which boat is 2 kilometres South of Dorothy?

W **6** **Do Workbook Page 8.**

7 (a) Draw a grid like this on squared paper.
Mark the points with co-ordinates (1,1), (5,1), and (3,6).
Join the points in the order given, then join the first to
the last. Name the shape you have drawn.
(b) Do all this again, on a new grid, for the points
(0,3), (3,4), (6,3), and (3,2).
(c) Repeat for the points
(2,6), (4,6), (6,3), (4,0), (2,0), and (0,3).

Ask your teacher if you should do Co-ordinate Cards 21, 23, 25, 27, 29.

Area of a rectangle

1 Find the area of each rectangle in **squares**.

(a) 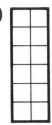   **(b)** 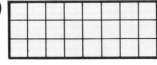   **(c)**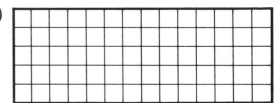

2 **(a)** How many squares are there in **each row** of this rectangle?
   (b) How many rows are there?
   (c) What is the area of the rectangle in squares?

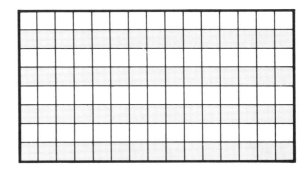

3 **Do Workbook Page 9.**

W

4 Find the area of each shape in squares.

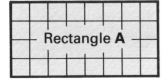
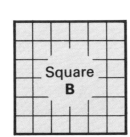
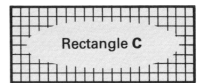

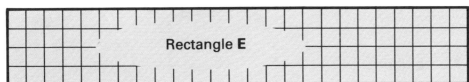

5 What is the area of each rectangle in squares?

(a)   **(b)**   **(c)**

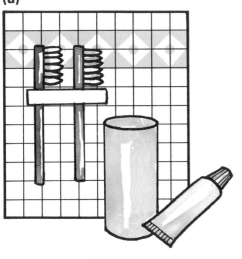

Making rectangles

1 (a) This rectangle is drawn on centimetre squared paper. How many squares are there in each row?
(b) How many rows are there?
(c) What is the area of the rectangle in square centimetres?

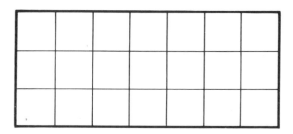

You need centimetre squared paper.

2 (a) The drawing shows the first row of centimetre squares in a rectangle. Copy this row on centimetre squared paper.
(b) Complete and colour the rectangle so that it has an area of 32 cm².

3 Repeat question **2** for rectangles with these first rows and areas:

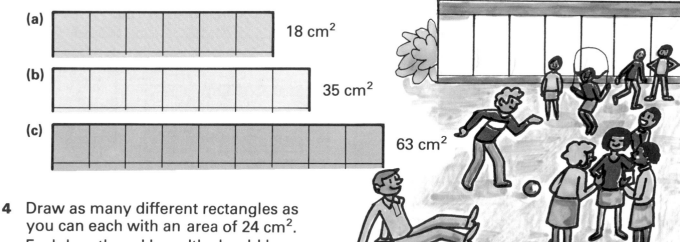

(a) 18 cm²

(b) 35 cm²

(c) 63 cm²

4 Draw as many different rectangles as you can each with an area of 24 cm². Each length and breadth should be a whole number of centimetres.

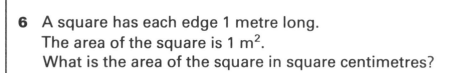

You need chalk and a long metric tape or trundle wheel.
Work in the playground with a partner.

5 (a) Mark out a rectangle with length 5 metres and breadth 3 metres.
(b) Draw a metre square in one corner.
(c) What is the area of the rectangle?
(d) Is the area of the rectangle more or less than the area of your classroom floor?

6 A square has each edge 1 metre long. The area of the square is 1 m². What is the area of the square in square centimetres?

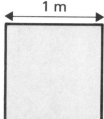

1 m

Finding areas

1 The red shape has been divided into two rectangles and a square. Copy and complete:

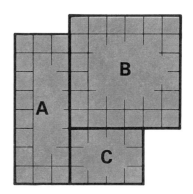

Area of rectangle **A** = _____ squares
Area of square **B** = _____ squares
Area of rectangle **C** = _____ squares

Area of the whole shape = _____ squares

2 Repeat question **1** to find the area of each whole shape.

(a)

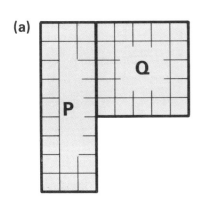

(b)

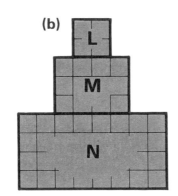

(c)

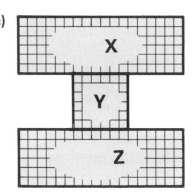

3 **Do Workbook Page 10.**

4 What is the area, in squares, of the yellow part of each bag?

(a)   (b)   (c)

Ask your teacher what to do next.

Millilitres

One litre has the same volume as 1000 millilitres.
1 litre = 1000 ml

1 Copy and complete:

(a) ½ litre = ½ of 1000 ml = _____ ml,   (b) ¼ litre = ¼ of 1000 ml = _____ ml.

2 These litre measuring jugs have a scale showing millilitres.

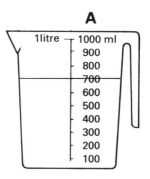 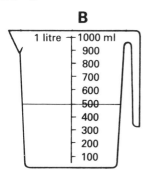 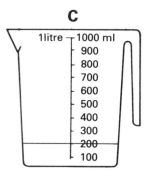 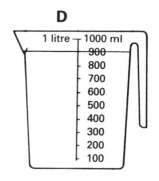

(a) What volume is shown by the level of liquid in each jug?

(b) Which jugs contain a volume of liquid greater than half a litre?

(c) Which jug contains a volume of liquid less than a quarter of a litre?

3 This diagram shows part of a scale on a measuring jar.

(a) How many small intervals are there between the 400 ml and the 500 ml marks?

(b) What volume does each small interval represent?

(c) What volume of liquid is there in this jar?

4 What volume of liquid is in each of these jars?

(a) 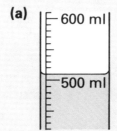 (b) 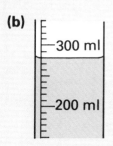 (c) 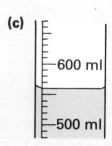 (d)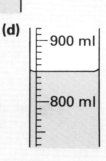

W **5** **Do Workbook Page 4, question 1.**

6 What volume of liquid is in each of these jars?

(a) 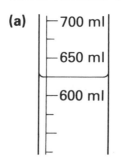 (b) 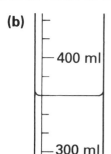 (c) 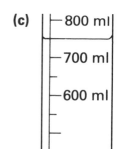 (d)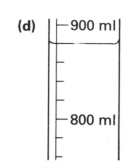

Reading to the nearest mark

1 Copy and complete these sentences for each jug:

(a) Jug **A** holds more than _____ ml and less than _____ ml.

(b) Jug **B** holds less than _____ ml and more than _____ ml.

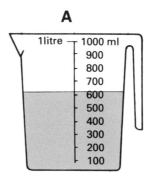

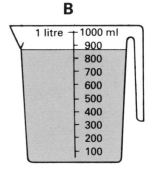

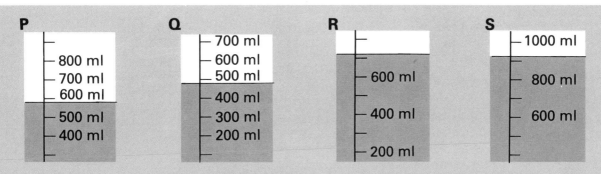

2 The volume in container **P** is 600 ml to the nearest 100 ml.
Write the volumes in containers **Q**, **R**, and **S to the nearest 100 ml**.

3 Read the volumes of these containers which have been emptied into the measuring jars:

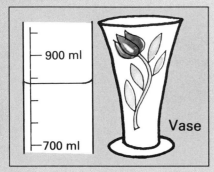

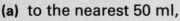

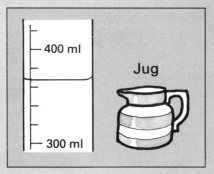

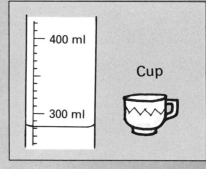

(a) to the nearest 50 ml,   (b) to the nearest mark,   (c) to the nearest mark.

4 **Ask for the small containers.**

(a) Fill one container with water.
Pour the water into a measuring jar.
Write the volume of the container using '**to the nearest**'.

(b) Do this again for the other containers.

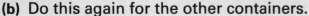

Litres and millilitres

1 **(a)** Which jar has a volume of $\frac{1}{4}$ litre?
(b) Which jar has a volume of $\frac{1}{2}$ litre?

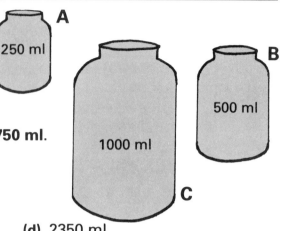

The three jars have a total volume of 1750 ml.

$\qquad$ 1750 ml = 1000 ml + 750 ml

The volume **1750 ml** can be written as **1 litre 750 ml**.

2 Write each of these volumes in the other way:
(a) 1150 ml $\qquad$ **(b)** 1485 ml $\qquad$ **(c)** 1060 ml $\qquad$ **(d)** 2350 ml
(e) 1 litre 230 ml $\qquad$ **(f)** 1 litre 80 ml $\qquad$ **(g)** 2 litres 820 ml $\qquad$ **(h)** 2 litres 5 ml

W **3** Do Workbook Page 4, question 3.

You need a 1 litre measuring jar and bottle P.

4 **(a)** Use a measuring jar to measure these three
volumes of water, and pour each into bottle **P**. | 400 ml | | 650 ml | | 950 ml |
(b) Calculate the total volume of water in
bottle **P**, and write your answer in two ways.
(c) Use the measuring jar to check your calculation.

5 **Ask for the large containers.**
(a) Fill one container with water.
Pour the water into a measuring jar.
Write the volume of the container using '**to the nearest**'.
(b) Do this again for the other containers.

6 A jug **J** was filled from measuring jar **M** which
held 1 litre of orange juice.
(a) What volume of orange juice is left
in measuring jar **M**?
(b) What is the volume of jug **J**?
(c) Use this method to find the volumes
of other containers which have a
volume less than 1 litre.

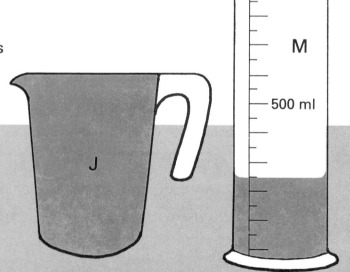

Ask your teacher what to do next.

Seconds

When measuring time we sometimes need a unit shorter than a minute.

This unit is called a **second**.

> 1 minute is **60 seconds**.

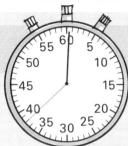

The **red** hand on this stop-watch shows **seconds**.
The stop-watch shows **38 seconds** have passed since it was started.

1   Find how many seconds have passed since each stop-watch or stop-clock was started.

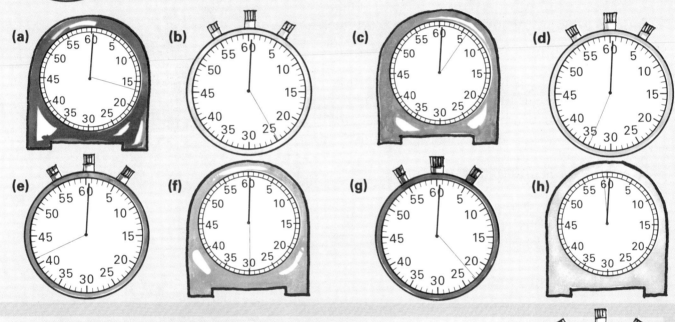

(a)   (b)   (c)   (d)

(e)   (f)   (g)   (h)

The **red** hand on the stop-watch shows **42 seconds**.
The **black** hand points to between 3 and 4 minutes.
3 minutes 42 seconds have passed since the stop-watch was started.

2   Find what time has passed since each stop-watch or stop-clock was started.

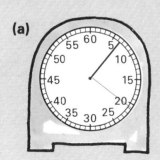
(a)

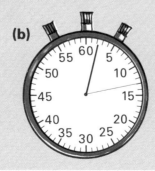
(b)

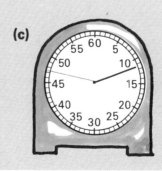
(c)

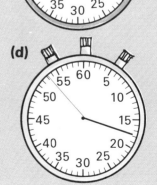
(d)

Timing yourself

Work with a partner.

You need a watch which measures time in seconds.

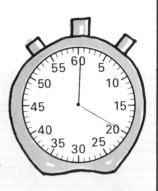

`0:00 20`

1 (a) Open a reading book. Read for 20 seconds.
Record the number of words you read.
   (b) Do this again.
   (c) How many words did you read **altogether**?
   (d) What was the **average** number of words you read in 20 seconds?

2 Write the numbers **1, 2, 3, 4, 5,** . . . and so on, for 40 seconds.
What number did you reach?

3 (a) Find out how many times you can write your first name in 30 seconds.
   (b) How many times do you think you could write your name in **1 minute**?

You need a long measuring tape or a trundle wheel.

Work in the school hall or the playground.

4 (a) **Estimate** how far you can walk at your
normal walking pace in 15 seconds.
   (b) Now **measure** how far you can walk in 15 seconds.
   (c) **Calculate** how far you could walk in **1 minute**.

5 Do question **4** again for **hopping**.

The stop-watch shows that David took
2 minutes 13 seconds to walk 200 metres.

`0:02 13`

Work in the playground.

6 Find your time in minutes and seconds to walk
   (a) 200 metres,
   (b) once round the perimeter of the playground.

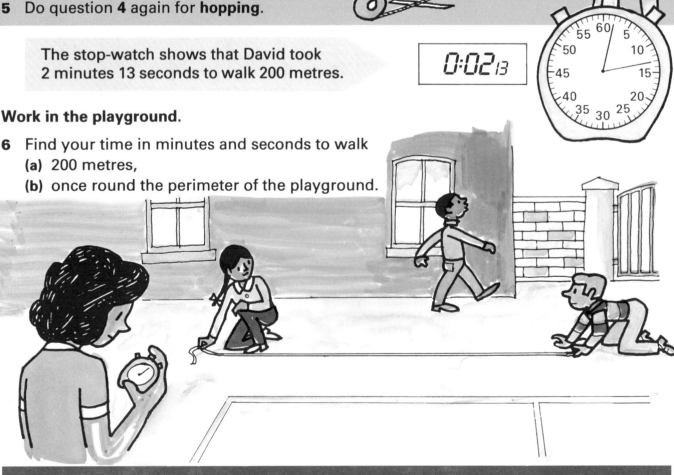

Athletics times

The digital stop-watch shows the time taken by the runner who won a 3000 metre race.

It was **9 minutes 17 seconds.**

1 **(a)** The second runner finished 10 seconds later. What was his time for the race?
   (b) The last runner finished 40 seconds after the winner. How long did he take?

2 Here are the finishing times of the first four runners in a 5000 metre race:

Rob `0:14 31`   Steve `0:14 12`

Ted `0:14 50`   Paul `0:14 19`

   (a) List the 1st, 2nd, and 3rd runners in the race with their times like this:

   1st _Steve_____   __14__ minutes __12__ seconds

   (b) How many seconds slower than the winner was the fourth runner?

Don won the marathon in a time of 2 hours 18 minutes 3 seconds.   `2:18 03`

Ivor `2:18 42`   Neil `2:21 14`

Joan `2:27 38`   Zena `2:27 51`

3 **(a)** Write the finishing times for each runner in hours, minutes, and seconds.
   (b) How much longer did Ivor take than Don?
   (c) How long after Don finished did Neil finish?
   (d) How many seconds was Zena behind Joan?

The table shows times in seconds and tenths of a second for the winners at a sports meeting.

	Men	Women
100 metres	10·5	11·4
200 metres	21·3	23·1
400 metres	46·7	50·2

4 **(a)** How much quicker was the men's 200 metres time than the women's?
   (b) How many seconds slower was the women's 400 metres time than the men's?
   (c) Find the difference between the times of the men's and women's 100 metres.

Ask your teacher what to do next.

Nets of cubes

W **1** Make templates with the shapes on **Workbook Page 20**.

2 **(a)** Use the **square template**.
Draw the net of a cube like this ➔

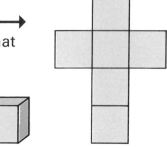

(b) Cut out your net. Fold it to check that it makes a cube.

(c) Stick the net in your jotter.

There are other nets of a cube.
Each net is a pattern of 6 squares

W **3** **(a)** Cut out each pattern from **Workbook Page 22**.
(b) Fold each pattern to find if it makes a cube.
(c) Stick in your jotter those nets which make cubes.

4 **(a)** Find another net of a cube which is different from those you have already made.
Do this by drawing on squared paper.
(b) Stick this new net in your jotter.

Nets of cuboids

This is a net of a cuboid.

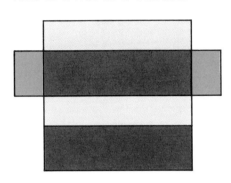

cuboid

1 **(a)** How many faces has a cuboid?
   (b) What is the shape of each face?
   (c) How many different sizes of faces are there?

There are other nets of a cuboid.

2 **(a)** Cut out each pattern from **Workbook Page 20**.
   (b) Fold each pattern to find if it makes a cuboid.
   (c) Stick in your jotter those nets which make cuboids.

3 **(a)** Use the **square template** and the **rectangle template**.
   Draw the net of a cuboid like this ——————▶
   (b) Cut out your net. Fold it to
   check that it makes a cuboid.

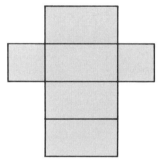

W

4 **(a)** Use the net you made in question **3**.
   (b) Cut off one **square** and join it in a
   different place as shown.
   (c) Fold the pattern to find if it makes a
   cuboid or not.

5 **(a)** Now move one **rectangle** as shown.
   (b) Does this new pattern
   make a cuboid?

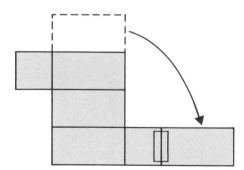

Nets of prisms

This is a net of a triangular prism ⟶

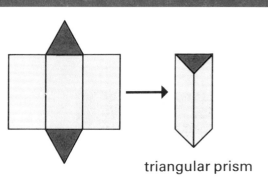

triangular prism

1 **(a)** How many faces has a triangular prism?
(b) Name the two different shapes
which make the net.

2 **(a)** Use the **rectangle template** and the **equilateral triangle template**.
Draw the net of a triangular prism as shown above.
(b) Cut out your net. Fold it to check that it makes a triangular prism.

There are other nets of a triangular prism.

3 **(a)** Use the net you made in question **2**.
(b) Cut off one triangle and join it
in a different place as shown.
(c) Fold the pattern to find if it
makes a triangular prism.
(d) Stick this net in your jotter.

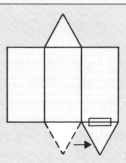

4 **(a)** Use the **square template** and the **equilateral triangle template**.

Draw this pattern.

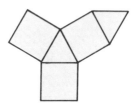

(b) Cut out your pattern. Fold it to find whether
it makes a triangular prism.
(c) Cut off one shape and join it in
a different place.
(d) Does this new pattern make a triangular prism?

5 **(a)** Use the templates to draw these five shapes:

(b) Cut them out. Join the shapes together to make
a net for a triangular prism like this

(c) Stick the net in your jotter.

Nets of pyramids

This is a net of a triangular pyramid ⟶

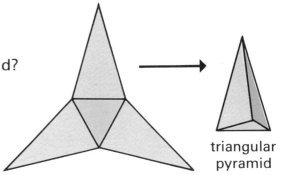

triangular pyramid

1 **(a)** How many faces has a triangular pyramid?
  (b) Name the two different triangles which make this net.

2 **(a)** Use the templates to draw the net shown above.
  (b) Cut out your net. Fold it to check that it makes a triangular pyramid.

3 **(a)** Use the net you made in question **2**. Cut off one triangle and join it in a different place.
  (b) Fold the pattern to find if it makes a triangular pyramid.

4 **(a)** Use the **square template** and the **isosceles triangle template**.

  Draw this pattern.

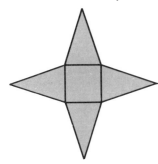

  (b) Cut out your pattern. Fold it to check that it makes a **square pyramid**.
  (c) Cut off one shape and join it in a different place.
  (d) Fold the pattern to see if it makes a square pyramid.
  (e) Stick the net in your jotter.

5 Name the shape which can be made from each net.

(a) 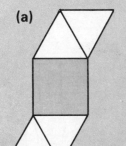   **(b)** 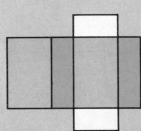   **(c)** 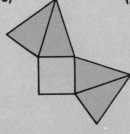   **(d)**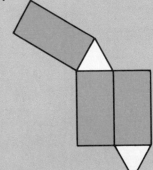

(e) 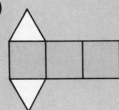   **(f)**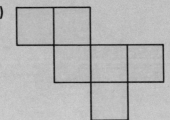

Ask your teacher what to do next.

SCHOOL
STOP

Part 2 Acknowledgements

p42. Oxprint
p47. Allsport (x2)
p48. Associated Sports Photography (x2)
p51. Oxprint
p60. P. Kemmett

Part 2

Adding and subtracting fractions

1 **(a)** For the flag,
write the fractions
coloured red, yellow,
and green.
Repeat this for
(b) the windbreak,
(c) the sunshade,
(d) the mat.

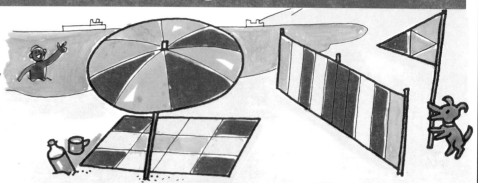

The dot on this number line shows $\frac{3}{8}$.

2 What fraction is shown by the dot on each of these number lines?

(a)    **(b)**    **(c)**

(d)    **(e)**    **(f)**

A **jump** of $\frac{3}{8}$ is shown
on each of these number lines,

3 What jump is shown on each of these number lines?

(a)    **(b)**    **(c)**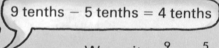

(d)   **(e)**   **(f)**

W **4** Do Workbook Page 17.

5

Addition

3 tenths + 4 tenths = 7 tenths

We write $\frac{3}{10} + \frac{4}{10}$
$= \frac{7}{10}$

Subtraction

9 tenths − 5 tenths = 4 tenths

We write $\frac{9}{10} - \frac{5}{10}$
$= \frac{4}{10}$

Copy and complete:

(a) $\frac{3}{5} + \frac{1}{5}$ **(b)** $\frac{7}{10} + \frac{2}{10}$ **(c)** $\frac{1}{3} + \frac{1}{3}$ **(d)** $\frac{1}{4} + \frac{2}{4}$ **(e)** $\frac{1}{6} + \frac{3}{6}$ **(f)** $\frac{3}{8} + \frac{4}{8}$ **(g)** $\frac{1}{10} + \frac{4}{10}$

(h) $\frac{9}{10} - \frac{1}{10}$ **(i)** $\frac{7}{8} - \frac{1}{8}$ **(j)** $\frac{3}{5} - \frac{2}{5}$ **(k)** $\frac{5}{6} - \frac{3}{6}$ **(l)** $\frac{2}{3} - \frac{1}{3}$ **(m)** $\frac{5}{8} - \frac{3}{8}$ **(n)** $\frac{7}{10} - \frac{3}{10}$

6 Copy and complete: **Remember:** $1 = \frac{2}{2}$; $1 = \frac{3}{3}$; $1 = \frac{4}{4}$; ...

(a) $\frac{3}{8} + \frac{\blacksquare}{8} = 1$ **(b)** $\frac{\blacksquare}{5} + \frac{1}{5} = 1$ **(c)** $\frac{5}{6} + \frac{\blacksquare}{6} = 1$ **(d)** $\frac{5}{10} + \frac{\blacksquare}{10} = 1$ **(e)** $\frac{1}{3} + \frac{\blacksquare}{3} = 1$

7 Copy and complete:

(a) $1 - \frac{3}{6} = \frac{\blacksquare}{\blacksquare}$ **(b)** $1 - \frac{2}{5} = \frac{\blacksquare}{\blacksquare}$ **(c)** $1 - \frac{9}{10} = \frac{\blacksquare}{\blacksquare}$ **(d)** $1 - \frac{6}{8} = \frac{\blacksquare}{\blacksquare}$ **(e)** $1 - \frac{1}{4} = \frac{\blacksquare}{\blacksquare}$

Wholes and fractions

On the shelf there are
2 whole tarts and $\frac{5}{8}$ of a tart.

There are $2\frac{5}{8}$ tarts altogether.

1 How many cakes altogether are shown in each picture?

(a)  (b)  (c)

2 How much is coloured in each of the following?

(a) 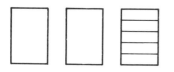 (b)

(c) (d) (e)

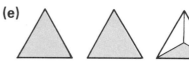

The coloured part of this scale shows $3\frac{1}{4}$.

3 How much is coloured on each of these scales?

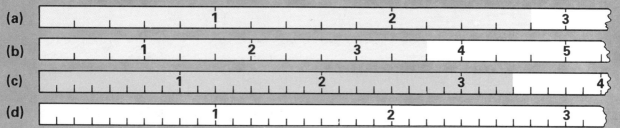

(a)

(b)

(c)

(d)

4 Do Workbook Pages 18 and 19. W

5 Copy and complete:

(a) $3\frac{2}{5} + \frac{1}{5}$ (b) $1\frac{4}{10} + 3\frac{3}{10}$ (c) $1\frac{1}{8} + \frac{4}{8}$ (d) $3\frac{1}{3} + 2\frac{1}{3}$ (e) $3\frac{2}{6} + \frac{1}{6}$ (f) $2\frac{1}{4} + 1\frac{1}{4}$

(g) $4\frac{1}{3} + 3$ (h) $5\frac{5}{8} + 2\frac{1}{8}$ (i) $\frac{1}{6} + 4\frac{1}{6}$ (j) $3\frac{1}{10} + \frac{7}{10}$ (k) $\frac{2}{5} + 4\frac{2}{5}$ (l) $5\frac{3}{10} + \frac{1}{10}$

6 Copy and complete:

(a) $3\frac{7}{10} - \frac{1}{10}$ (b) $6\frac{3}{5} - \frac{1}{5}$ (c) $4\frac{2}{3} - 1\frac{1}{3}$ (d) $4\frac{7}{8} - 3\frac{3}{8}$ (e) $3\frac{5}{6} - 1\frac{3}{6}$ (f) $5\frac{3}{4} - 1\frac{1}{4}$

(g) $5\frac{4}{5} - \frac{2}{5}$ (h) $7\frac{3}{8} - 1\frac{1}{8}$ (i) $4\frac{3}{6} - \frac{1}{6}$ (j) $7\frac{9}{10} - 2\frac{7}{10}$ (k) $3\frac{2}{3} - 3$ (l) $8\frac{7}{10} - 1\frac{7}{10}$

7

Pointer **A** shows the weight of an empty bucket.
Pointer **B** shows the weight of the bucket filled with water.
What is the weight of the water?

Ask your teacher what to do next.

Revision

| Find 36 ÷ 4 ⟶ | 36 ÷ 4 = **9**   because 4 × **9** = 36 |

1   Write the answers for:
   (a) 18 ÷ 3   (b) 35 ÷ 5   (c) 40 ÷ 8   (d) 36 ÷ 9   (e) 56 ÷ 7   (f) 54 ÷ 6
   (g) 32 ÷ 4   (h) 64 ÷ 8   (i) 24 ÷ 6   (j) 81 ÷ 9   (k) 27 ÷ 3   (l) 63 ÷ 7

Find 38 ÷ 4.   4 times what is about 38?   4 times 9 is 36.   36 and 2 make 38.   38 ÷ 4 is 9 remainder 2.

2   (a) 46 ÷ 9   (b) 17 ÷ 2   (c) 48 ÷ 5   (d) 50 ÷ 8   (e) 47 ÷ 7   (f) 26 ÷ 3
   (g) 78 ÷ 9   (h) 35 ÷ 8   (i) 51 ÷ 7   (j) 23 ÷ 4   (k) 52 ÷ 6   (l) 66 ÷ 9

3   (a) 30 ÷ 5   (b) 21 ÷ 2   (c) 43 ÷ 6   (d) 27 ÷ 8   (e) 54 ÷ 9   (f) 22 ÷ 3
   (g) 36 ÷ 6   (h) 30 ÷ 7   (i) 37 ÷ 7   (j) 58 ÷ 8   (k) 90 ÷ 9   (l) 42 ÷ 8

4   (a)   Which of these numbers when divided by 9 have a remainder of 1?
   (b)   Which of these numbers when divided by 8 have a remainder of 2?

55   82   42   34   73   64

| Find $\frac{1}{8}$ of 80 ⟶ | $\frac{1}{8}$ **of 80**   is the same as   **80 ÷ 8** ⟶ | $\frac{1}{8}$ of 80 = 10 |

5   (a) $\frac{1}{3}$ of 12   (b) $\frac{1}{6}$ of 30   (c) $\frac{1}{9}$ of 27   (d) $\frac{1}{4}$ of 28   (e) $\frac{1}{5}$ of 45   (f) $\frac{1}{7}$ of 70

6   Sally and Tommy have 42 cards to pin on a board.
   (a) How many groups of 6 cards could they make?
   (b) If they put the cards into 7 equal groups, how many would be in each group?
   (c) How many rows of 9 could they make and how many cards would be left over?
   (d) If the cards are put into 8 equal rows, what is the greatest number there can be in each row? How many would be left over?
   (e) They put the cards in groups of 5. How many groups did they have? How many more cards did they need to make another group of 5?

PIGEONS RACING TODAY

Dividing hundreds and thousands

To find **8883 ÷ 7**	Share the 8 thousands ⟶	8 ÷ 7 = 1 remainder 1	$\dfrac{1}{7\,|\,8^18\,8\,3}$
	Share the 18 hundreds ⟶	18 ÷ 7 = 2 remainder 4	$\dfrac{1\ 2}{7\,|\,8^18^48\,3}$
	Share the 48 tens ⟶	48 ÷ 7 = 6 remainder 6	$\dfrac{1\ 2\ 6}{7\,|\,8^18^48^63}$
	Share the 63 units ⟶	63 ÷ 7 = 9	$\dfrac{1\ 2\ 6\ 9}{7\,|\,8^18^48^63}$

1
(a) 2|3956   (b) 5|7130   (c) 4|528   (d) 3|6639   (e) 6|834
(f) 6|8952   (g) 3|834   (h) 7|8393   (i) 7|903   (j) 8|9968

2
(a) 9536 ÷ 8   (b) 900 ÷ 5   (c) 9436 ÷ 7   (d) 963 ÷ 9   (e) 2688 ÷ 3
(f) 8072 ÷ 8   (g) 8036 ÷ 4   (h) 9045 ÷ 5   (i) 9810 ÷ 9   (j) 9872 ÷ 8

To find **5439 ÷ 9**	Share the 5 thousands ⟶	There are not enough.	
	Share the 54 hundreds ⟶	54 ÷ 9 = 6	$\dfrac{6}{9\,|\,5\,4\,3\,9}$
	Share the 3 tens ⟶	3 ÷ 9 = 0 remainder 3	$\dfrac{6}{9\,|\,5\,4\,3^39}$
	Share the 39 units ⟶	39 ÷ 9 = 4 remainder 3	$\dfrac{6\ 0\ 4\ \text{r}3}{9\,|\,5\,4\,3^39}$

3
(a) 4|2325   (b) 6|4639   (c) 8|8859   (d) 9|3459   (e) 3|2425
(f) 8|5597   (g) 9|9973   (h) 5|4038   (i) 7|5858   (j) 9|4626

4
(a) 5331 ÷ 8   (b) 9254 ÷ 9   (c) 3474 ÷ 6   (d) 3603 ÷ 4   (e) 8480 ÷ 8

5
(a) Divide this number by 8.
(b) If this number was divided by 9, would the answer be **larger** or **smaller** than the answer for (a)?
(c) If this number was divided by 7, would the answer be **larger** or **smaller** than the answer for (a)?

6 (a) Pencils are packed in cases. Each case holds 8 pencils.
In one day 9000 pencils are packed. How many cases are used?
(b) A different case holds 7 pencils.
Would **more** or **less** of these cases be needed to pack 9000 pencils?
How many cases of 7 pencils can be filled?

7 Divide these numbers by 10:
(a) 4270   (b) 3090   (c) 4296   (d) 8792   (e) 5443   (f) 7166

Cost of one

1 (a) What is the cost of **one** Drunchie bar if you buy a packet of 5?
   (b) How much cheaper is this than the cost of the single bar?

2 Find the cost of **one** bar in each of these packets:

(a)    (b)    (c)

3 How much dearer is the single bar price than the price of one bar from a packet?

(a)    (b)    (c)

Find the cost of one can.
$$8\overline{)2\,5^16p}\quad 32p$$

One can costs **32p**.

4 Find the cost of one:

(a)    (b)    (c)

5 How much cheaper is one can from a pack than the price of the single can?

(a) LEMONADE one can **28p**   (b) COLA one can **29p**   (c) GINGER BEER one can **30p**
pack of 6 **£1·32**   pack of 6 **£1·68**   pack of 6 **£1·50**

How many 8p tickets can be bought for £3·60?

£3·60 is 360p.
$$8\overline{)3\,6^40}\quad 45$$

45 tickets can be bought.

6 How many (a) 9p tickets can be bought with £5·40,
           (b) 5p sweets can be bought with £3·75,
           (c) 6p lollipops can be bought with £5·04?

 Scout Fair  Homemade Cakes 8p each

 John collected £3·36

Ben collected £3·84

 Steve collected £4

7 How many cakes did each boy sell?

Division of large numbers

Use the calculator to find 5320 ÷ 8 like this.

Enter **5320.** Press **÷** **8** **=** to give **665.**

So 5320 ÷ 8 = **665**   Press **C** to clear the calculator.

1 Now do these divisions:
- **(a)** 5274 ÷ 9
- **(b)** 5404 ÷ 7
- **(c)** 5850 ÷ 6
- **(d)** 6723 ÷ 9
- **(e)** 9168 ÷ 4
- **(f)** 5369 ÷ 7
- **(g)** 4015 ÷ 5
- **(h)** 8712 ÷ 8
- **(i)** 4722 ÷ 6
- **(j)** 5008 ÷ 8

A calculator is very useful for dividing large numbers.

Find 62 976 ÷ 8 like this: Enter **62976.** Press **÷** **8** **=** to give **7872.**

You can check your answer in two ways:

Method 1 do the **division** again.

or **Method 2** do *not* clear the calculator, **multiply** your answer by 8.   **7872.** Press **×** **8** **=** to give **62976.**

2 Do these divisions. Write each answer and check it.
- **(a)** 39 336 ÷ 6
- **(b)** 73 773 ÷ 9
- **(c)** 54 824 ÷ 8
- **(d)** 288 484 ÷ 7
- **(e)** 471 267 ÷ 9
- **(f)** 790 120 ÷ 8
- **(g)** 88 710 ÷ 6
- **(h)** 3 995 508 ÷ 4
- **(i)** 840 537 ÷ 9
- **(j)** 1 812 741 ÷ 7

3 Caroline found there were 1980 words on 4 pages of a book.
What is the average number of words on a page?

4 Jane counted 2688 words on 8 pages of her book.
What is the average number of words on a page?

Here are the numbers of letters in 4 lines of a book: **46,   42,   48,   44.**
What is the average number of letters in a line?

Press **4** **6** **+** **4** **2** **+** **4** **8** **+** **4** **4** **=** to give   **180.**

Do **not** clear the calculator.   Press **÷** **4** **=** to give   **45.**

The average number of letters in a line is **45**.

5 These are the numbers of names in 6 columns in the telephone directory:
127,   125,   126,   123,   126,   129.
What is the average number of names in a column?

6 These are the numbers of pages in six books:
148,   232,   197,   256,   229,   186.
What is the average number of pages in a book?

Approximate answers

There are 213 children in the 7 classes of our school.
Find the average number of children in a class.

Aileen found the answer like this

$$\begin{array}{r} 3\,0\,\text{r}\,3 \\ 7\overline{)2\,1\,3} \end{array}$$

William used his calculator.
He noticed the decimal point

`30.428571`

Both wrote: The average number of children in a class is **about 30**.

Use a calculator for all the examples on this page.

1 Six children found they had a total of 140 pencils.
What is the average number of pencils for a child?

2 Eight children each wrote the number of letters in their name:
15, 12, 11, 16, 9, 11, 10, 13.
What is the average number of letters in a name?

3 Write the names of 7 classmates. Find the average number of letters for these names.

4 Nine children each wrote the number of cars they saw in their street:
32, 43, 27, 36, 40, 36, 29, 33, 31.
What is the average number of cars seen by a child?

5 Six children each took a handful of counters.
They counted how many they had:
18, 22, 33, 24, 19, 23.
Find the average number of counters in a handful.

6 Ask each of three classmates to take one handful of counters.
How many is their average handful?

7 Write **true** or **false** for these:
(a) 475 ÷ 3 has an answer about 158,
(b) 3698 ÷ 7 has an answer about 528,
(c) 1542 ÷ 9 has an answer about 17,
(d) 58 562 ÷ 6 has an answer about 97 603,
(e) 45 678 ÷ 9 has an answer about 5075.

8 How many
(a) packets of 8 biscuits can you make from 9145 biscuits,
(b) boxes of 6 cakes can you pack from 5120 cakes,
(c) cans holding 6 litres can be filled from 8000 litres,
(d) 3 kg bags can be made up from 2500 kg of salt,
(e) lengths of 9 metres can be cut from 8200 metres of cloth,
(f) rows of 7 seats can be made from one thousand seats,
(g) biscuits costing 7p can be bought with £2·50,
(h) lollipops costing 9p can be bought with £3?

Ask your teacher if you should do Number Cards 22, 24, 26, 28, 30.

Tenths and hundredths

---

7 **tenths** is written in decimal form as **0·7**

1 Write in decimal form:
(a) 3 tenths, (b) 1 tenth, (c) 9 tenths, (d) 6 tenths, (e) 5 tenths, (f) $\frac{4}{10}$, (g) $\frac{2}{10}$.

2 For each shape write, in decimal form, the fraction coloured and the fraction white.

(a) 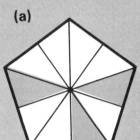 (b) 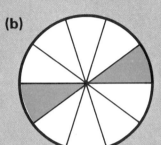 (c) 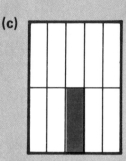 (d) 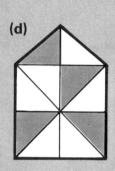 (e)

---

3 **units** and 7 **tenths** is written in decimal form as **3·7**

3 Write in decimal form:
(a) 5 units and 1 tenth, (b) 2 units and 4 tenths,
(c) 6 units and 9 tenths, (d) $1\frac{2}{10}$, (e) $9\frac{7}{10}$.

4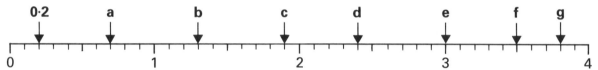

The first arrow shows 0·2. Write in decimal form what each of the other arrows show.

This square is divided into 100 equal parts.
Each **small** square is one hundredth ($\frac{1}{100}$) of the square.
In decimal form, **1 hundredth** is written as **0·01**, $\frac{7}{100}$ is written as **0·07**
                13 hundredths is written as **0·13**, $\frac{60}{100}$ is written as **0·60**

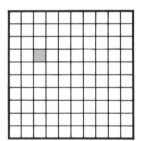

5 Write in decimal form:
(a) 31 hundredths, (b) 20 hundredths, (c) 2 hundredths,
(d) $\frac{87}{100}$, (e) $\frac{9}{100}$, (f) $\frac{40}{100}$.

0·13 is equal to **13 hundredths**.

6 Write these in the same way: (a) 0·41 (b) 0·67 (c) 0·59 (d) 0·09

0·60 is equal to $\frac{60}{100}$.

7 Write these in the same way: (a) 0·90 (b) 0·03 (c) 0·11 (d) 0·30

Do Workbook Page 11, questions 1 and 2.

W

Wholes and hundredths

1 For each square write, in decimal form, the fraction shown by each colour.
Record like this **(a)** 0·35, 0·65

(a) 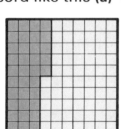 **(b)** 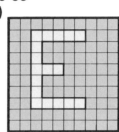 **(c)** 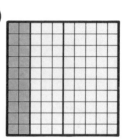 **(d)**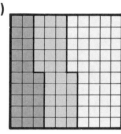

2 Here is a number line from 0 to 1 divided into hundredths:

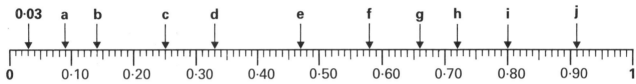

The first arrow shows 0·03. Write in decimal form what each of the other arrows shows.

3 Write in order, starting with the **smallest**: 0·21, 0·16, 0·27, 0·61, 0·12, 0·72

4 Write in order, starting with the **largest**: 0·39, 0·22, 0·33, 0·08, 0·80, 0·93

1 whole square and 28 hundredths of the other is coloured.

In decimal form, **1 unit and 28 hundredths** is written as **1·28**

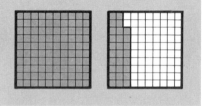

5 For each diagram write, in decimal form,
the amount coloured.

(a) 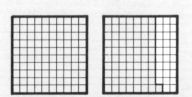 **(b)**

(c) 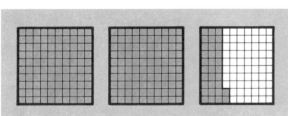 **(d)**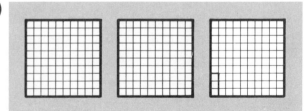

6 Write in decimal form: **(a)** 8 units and 11 hundredths, **(b)** 2 units and 22 hundredths,
(c) 3 units and 30 hundredths, **(d)** 1 unit and 3 hundredths,
(e) $5\frac{5}{100}$, **(f)** $6\frac{40}{100}$.

7 Write in order, starting with the **smallest**: 0·31, 0·13, 1·03, 3·01, 1·30

8 Write in order, starting with the **largest**: 1·10, 0·11, 10·10, 0·10, 1·01

Using hundredths

100p = £1
1 penny is **one hundredth** of £1.

1p = £0·01

42p is 42 hundredths of £1 = £0·42   £3 and 42 pence is £3·42

1 In the same way write in £s:
(a) 16p   (b) 43p   (c) 7p   (d) 83p   (e) 8p   (f) 50p   (g) 70p
(h) £5 and 73 pence   (i) £7 and 40 pence   (j) £8 and 5 pence   (k) £2 and 22 pence

£0·03 is 3 hundredths of £1 = 3p   £2·03 is £2 and 3 pence

2 In the same way write as pence or as pounds and pence:
(a) £0·39   (b) £0·20   (c) £0·05   (d) £0·91   (e) £5·75   (f) £4·30   (g) £7·77

3 Write in £s the prices shown:

SOUP 27p   COFFEE 99p   JAM 58p   SWEETS 9p   CAKE 89p   BUTTER 62p   TEA 56p

100 cm = 1 m   1 centimetre is **one hundredth** of 1 metre.

1 cm = 0·01 m

31 cm is 31 hundredths of 1 metre = 0·31 m   5 m 31 cm is 5·31 m

4 In the same way write these lengths in metres:
(a) 23 cm   (b) 17 cm   (c) 80 cm   (d) 8 cm   (e) 95 cm   (f) 5 cm   (g) 50 cm
(h) 3 m 83 cm   (i) 7 m 60 cm   (j) 5 m 2 cm   (k) 1 m 11 cm   (l) 2 m 20 cm

0·84 m is 84 hundredths of 1 metre = 84 cm   5·84 m is 5 m 84 cm

5 In the same way write these in centimetres or in metres and centimetres:
(a) 0·39 m   (b) 0·03 m   (c) 0·50 m   (d) 0·95 m   (e) 5·20 m   (f) 3·06 m   (g) 5·55 m

6 The heights of six children are:
Adam 1·35 m   John 1·06 m   Jani 1·60 m
Alan 0·96 m   Mira 1·53 m   Pam 1·16 m
(a) List the heights from shortest to tallest.
(b) Who is shorter than 1 metre?
(c) Which children are taller than $1\frac{1}{2}$ metres?

Tenths and hundredths

10 hundredths coloured

1 tenth coloured

10 hundredths ⟷ 1 tenth

37 hundredths coloured

3 tenths and 7 hundredths coloured

37 hundredths ⟷ 3 tenths and 7 hundredths

1 Write each of these like this   0·49 = 49 hundredths = 4 tenths and 9 hundredths

(a) 0·51   (b) 0·19   (c) 0·91   (d) 0·70   (e) 0·08   (f) 0·33   (g) 0·07

2 Write each of these like this   35·28 = 3 tens 5 units 2 tenths and 8 hundredths

(a) 32·15   (b) 3·84   (c) 5·02   (d) 48·60   (e) 210·69   (f) 508·05

3 Write the **value** of each red digit:
(a) 76·2   (b) 3·04   (c) 257·51   (d) 0·43

7 tenths and 2 hundredths is written in decimal form as **0·72**

4 Write in decimal form:
(a) 3 tenths and 4 hundredths,   (b) 6 tenths and 5 hundredths,
(c) 1 tenth and 7 hundredths,   (d) 0 tenths and 9 hundredths.

5

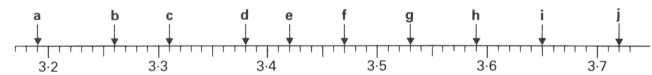

The first arrow shows 0·08. Write in decimal form what each other arrow shows.

6 Here is part of a number line:

Write in decimal form what each arrow shows.

7 Which of the following numbers are **between** 4·5 and 5·4?

4·44   5·45   4·55   5·14   5·04   5·41   4·05   4·95

W **Do Workbook Page 11, questions 4 to 7, and Workbook Page 12.**

Adding tenths and hundredths

9 tenths + 4 tenths = 13 tenths = 1·3

1 Do these in the same way:
(a) 8 tenths + 6 tenths   (b) 7 tenths + 8 tenths   (c) 9 tenths + 8 tenths

2 Add:

(a) 0·8
     0·3

(b) 0·9
     0·9

(c) 0·7
     0·3
     0·9

(d) 1·5
     0·4
     0·7

(e) 3·7
     4·2
     1·1

3 The marks given by six judges in a skating competition were: 5·6, 5·5, 5·7, 5·8, 5·4, 5·5. The highest and lowest marks are not counted. Find the skater's total mark by adding together the other four marks.

7 hundredths + 5 hundredths = 12 hundredths
                            = 1 tenth + 2 hundredths

4 Do these in the same way:
(a) 6 hundredths + 7 hundredths
(b) 5 hundredths + 9 hundredths   (c) 3 hundredths + 7 hundredths

7 hundredths and 8 hundredths are 15 hundredths. 15 hundredths is 1 tenth and 5 hundredths. . . . .

     0·38
   +0·27
     0·65

5
(a)   0·19
    +0·65

(b)   6·24
    +0·57

(c)   2·18
    +3·91

(d)   8·75
    +5·47

(e)   0·34
      0·18
    +0·25

(f)   4·27
      3·48
    +0·15

(g)   7·64
     12·03
    +0·75

36p + £1·85 can be found like this:
     £0·36
     £1·85
     £2·21

6 Find the cost of
(a) the cheapest 3 course meal,
(b) the dearest 3 course meal,
(c) your own choice of 3 course meal.

Menu

Soup	55p
Juice	35p
Egg & Chips	£2·55
Steak & Chips	£3·99
Chicken & Chips	£3·49
Apple Tart	78p
Ice Cream	37p
Trifle	95p

Subtracting tenths and hundredths

4·6 = 4 units and 6 tenths = 3 units and 16 tenths

1 Do these in the same way:
(a) 5·3   (b) 6·2   (c) 2·8   (d) 1·5   (e) 9·7   (f) 3·6   (g) 8·1   (h) 5·0

2 Find:

(a)	(b)	(c)	(d)	(e)	(f)	(g)	(h)
8·2	9·1	7·2	14·3	28·1	31·2	53·5	80·0
−0·7	−6·8	−6·9	−3·5	−13·6	−16·4	−47·7	−74·2

3 Mr Jones weighs 64·6 kg, his daughter Gwen weighs 37·3 kg, and his son Dai weighs 27·9 kg.
(a) How much heavier is Mr Jones than Gwen?
(b) How much lighter is Dai than Gwen?
(c) Do Gwen and Dai together weigh more than their father?

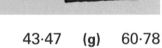

6 hundredths take away 2 hundredths is 4 hundredths.
7 tenths take away 3 tenths is 4 tenths.

```
 0·76
−0·32
 0·44
```

4

(a)	(b)	(c)	(d)	(e)	(f)	(g)
0·78	0·99	3·87	9·85	17·38	43·47	60·78
−0·52	−0·16	−2·77	−5·81	−8·14	−21·42	−32·78

1 tenth can be exchanged for **10 hundredths.**

2 hundredths take away 5 hundredths. I cannot do this.
Exchange 1 tenth for 10 hundredths.
12 hundredths take away 5 hundredths is 7 hundredths.
3 tenths take away 2 tenths is 1 tenth.

```
  0·³4¹2
−0·2 5
 0·1 7
```

5 Find:

(a)	(b)	(c)	(d)	(e)	(f)	(g)
0·45	0·93	0·71	7·91	4·23	15·14	28·30
−0·18	−0·64	−0·65	−3·64	−2·86	−7·06	−17·68

6 Find the difference in the costs of:
(a) the sandals and the T-shirt,   (b) the shorts and the T-shirt,
(c) the sandals and the shorts.

7 Find the change from £10 when you buy:
(a) the sandals   (b) the T-shirt,
(c) the shorts.

Heights

You need a metre stick or a metric tape.
Work with a partner.

1 **(a)** Measure your height.
Record like this:
My height is about 1·43 m.
(b) Measure in metres and record the
length from finger tip to finger tip
with your arms outstretched.
(c) Measure in metres and record the
height from the floor to the highest
point on the wall you can reach.

152 cm can be written as 1·52 m

2 The picture shows the heights of a
family of acrobats.
Write the heights of the acrobats,
Pop, Mop, Flip, and Flop, in
centimetres and then in metres.

3 One acrobat stands on another
acrobat's head. Which pairs have a total
height of more than 3·50 m?

4 Find, in metres, the difference
between the heights of
(a) Pop and Mop, **(b)** Pop and Flip,
(c) Mop and Flop, **(d)** Flip and Flop.

5 Write in **metres**:
(a) the length of the piece of wood,
(b) the height of the plant pot,
(c) the height of the potted plant.

Sport

1 In an International 100 metres final the times, **in seconds**, were:

Russia 10·34   West Germany 10·47
Finland 10·49   East Germany 10·26
France 10·76   Great Britain 10·52

(a) List the countries in order from first to last.

(b) Find the difference between the times of the first and last.

2 In the 200 metres final, a runner was timed at 20·35 seconds. This was 67 hundredths of a second faster than in the heat. What was his time in the heat?

3 In the relay race, the four runners in a team had times of 11·34, 12·18, 11·47, and 11·23 seconds. Find the total time taken by this team.

4 Five athletes threw the javelin distances of 55·36 m, 51·97 m, 55·63 m, 53·56 m, 51·79 m.

(a) Which was the best throw?

(b) What was the difference between the best and worst throws?

(c) List the throws in order from best to worst.

5 In a heat of the 100 m race, a swimmer took 58·41 seconds. In the final, the swimmer was 7 hundredths of a second faster. What was this swimmer's time in the final?

6 **Use a calculator if you wish.**
Four divers each had three dives.
The points scored were:

	J. Bone	R. Watt	D. Gray	W. Green
1st dive	43·71	52·68	47·93	56·14
2nd dive	48·76	54·17	45·28	53·21
3rd dive	45·93	56·73	44·62	54·18

(a) Find who was leading after **two** dives.

(b) Find the total scored by each diver after **three** dives.

(c) List the divers in final order from first to last.

Ask your teacher what to do next.

Target answers

The numbers **2**, **4**, and **6** can be used to make different target answers.

Each number is used once only. The signs + − × ÷ can be used more than once. The bracket shows the part to be calculated first.

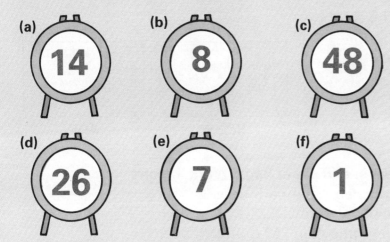

$(4 \times 6) - 2$ → **22**

$4 \times (6 - 2)$ → **16**

$(6 + 2) \div 4$ → **2**

1 Show how to make these targets using **2**, **4**, and **6**:

(a) **14** (b) **8** (c) **48**

(d) **26** (e) **7** (f) **1**

2 Use the numbers **3**, **5**, and **7** to make these targets:

(a) **22** (b) **16** (c) **2**

3 (a) Give your neighbour two targets for the numbers **3**, **5**, and **7**.
   (b) What is the highest possible target you can find for **3**, **5**, and **7**?
   (c) What is the lowest possible target you can find for **3**, **5**, and **7**?

4 Find **three different ways** of making this target using the numbers **2**, **3**, and **6**.

9

Ask your teacher if you should do Investigation Cards 32, 34, 36, 38, 40.

Kitchen and bathroom scales

1 **(a)** What does each small interval represent on this scale?
(b) What weight does each pointer show?

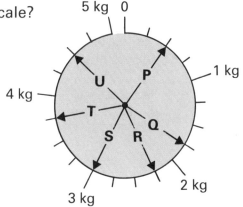

2 Repeat question 1 for this scale:

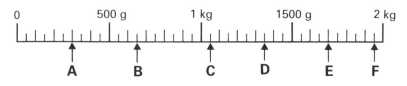

3 John went on a diet for 8 weeks. The scales show his weight before and after his diet.
(a) What was his weight before dieting?
(b) How much weight did he lose?
(c) On average, how many grams did he lose each week?

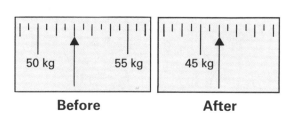

Before   **After**

4 **You need kitchen scales, butter beans, and paper bags. Work in pairs.**
(a) Weigh out 50 grams of beans in a bag. Your partner should check that the beans weigh 50 grams.
(b) In the same way, weigh out 100 grams then 250 grams of beans.
(c) What is the total weight of beans in the three bags?
(d) How much lighter than $\frac{1}{2}$ kilogram is this?

5 In a recipe for *Cherry Mallow Slice* chopped cherries and marshmallows are mixed with crushed biscuits and condensed milk. Find the weights of the:
(a) cherries,   **(b)** marshmallows,   **(c)** biscuits.

 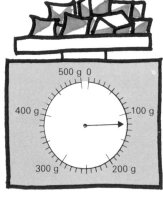 

6 Ask if you can make *Cherry Mallow Slice*.
Mix the ingredients together and then roll into a sausage shape, coat with chocolate vermicelli, cover in foil, and leave to set in a cool place before slicing and serving.

Ingredients

glacé cherries
marshmallows
digestive biscuits
small tin of
condensed milk
chocolate vermicelli

Weighing parcels

You need a two-pan balance,
100 g and 50 g weights, and
parcels **A**, **B**, **C**, and **D**.

1 (a) Copy and complete:
      Parcel **A** weighs more than _____ grams and less than _____ grams.
      Parcel **A** weighs between _____ grams and _____ grams.

  (b) **Weigh** parcels **B**, **C**, and **D** using 100 g and 50 g weights only.
      Write the weights as you did for parcel **A**.

  (c) These red kitchen scales show that parcel **A**
      weighs between 150 grams and 200 grams.

      Which parcel is being weighed on each scale below?
      Copy and complete:
      Parcel _____ is on the blue scale.
      Parcel _____ is on the green scale.
      Parcel _____ is on the orange scale.

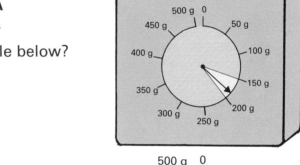

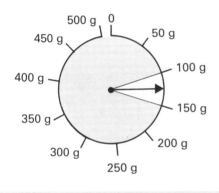 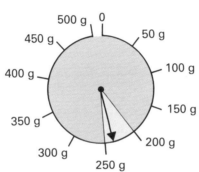 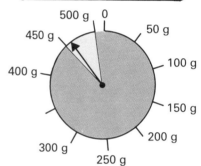

2 Each small interval represents 20 g on this scale ⟶
  Pointer **P** shows a weight **between 80 g and 100 g**.
  What weight does each pointer **Q**, **R**, **S**, **T**, and **U** show?

3 What weight does each pointer show on this scale?

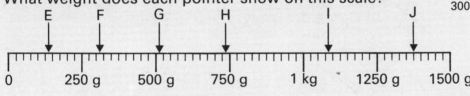

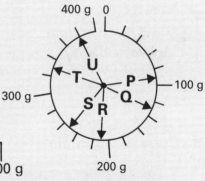

4 **You need kitchen scales and parcels A, B, C, and D.**
  (a) Weigh parcels **A**, **B**, **C**, and **D** as accurately as you can.
  (b) Do the same for some classroom objects.

5 **You need bathroom scales.**
  Work with a partner.

  Weigh **yourselves** in kilograms.
  Who is heavier and by how much?

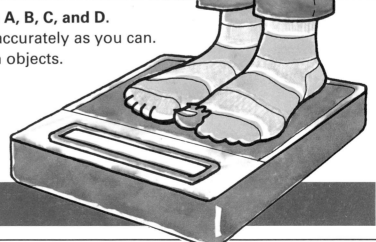

What do the contents weigh?

You need kitchen scales, a measuring jar, and water.

1 (a) Find the weight of the empty measuring jar.
   (b) Pour 1 litre of water into the jar.
       Find the total weight of the jar and the water.
   (c) **Calculate** the weight of the water. Copy and complete:
       The weight of 1 litre of water is about _____.

2 An empty bottle weighs 450 g. When filled with water it weighs 1 kg 440 g.
   (a) What is the weight of the water?
   (b) About what volume has the water?

3 An empty jar was placed on a
   kitchen scale and the pointer moved
   to the position marked **X**.
   The jar was then filled with water and
   the pointer moved to a new position **Y**.
   What is the weight of (a) the jar, (b) the jar and the water, (c) the water?

4 An empty bowl was placed on the scales and the pointer moved to position **P**.
   450 g of butter were added to the bowl.
   What was the scale reading then?

67g 454g 397g 500g 450g

net weights

On many containers you can see the words **net weight**.
The **net weight** is the weight of the **contents only**.
The **gross weight** is the total weight of the contents **and** the packaging.

Gross weight = net weight + weight of packaging

5 Copy and complete:

Gross weight	475 g	1 kg 350 g	2 kg 460 g			3 kg
Net weight	400 g	890 g		906 g	1 kg 875 g	
Weight of packaging	75 g		590 g	248 g	315 g	540 g

6 One sugar stick weighs 60 g. There are 120 sticks
   in a full box. The empty box weighs 300 g.
   (a) What is the net weight of the full box?
   (b) What is the gross weight of the full box?
   (c) What is the total weight of the box and sweets
       after 30 sugar sticks are sold?

Heavyweights

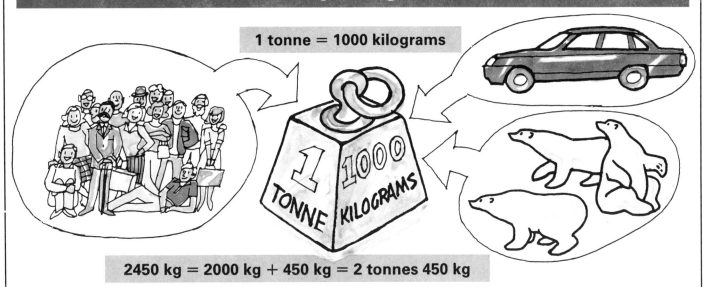

1 tonne = 1000 kilograms

2450 kg = 2000 kg + 450 kg = 2 tonnes 450 kg

1 Write these weights in tonnes and kilograms:
(a) African elephant – 5700 kilograms, (b) diplodocus – 10 560 kilograms.

2 Write these weights in kilograms:
(a) railway carriage – 35 tonnes, (b) submarine – 450 tonnes.

3 A truck weighs 4 tonnes and its load of gravel weighs 6500 kg. What is the total weight in tonnes and kilograms?

4 A lorry is carrying 120 bags of coal each weighing 50 kg. What is the total weight, in tonnes, of the coal?

Use a calculator if you wish.

5 A mint weighs about 1 gram.
About how many mints weigh 1 tonne?

6 Find the total weight of all the children in your class. By how many kilograms is this total weight more or less than 1 tonne?

7 (a) On average 15 adults have a total weight of about 1 tonne.
How many adults are there in your school?
Do you think that all the adults in your school together weigh more than, less than or about 1 tonne?

Find the number of adults who together would weigh about the same as:
(b) a double-decker bus – 12 000 kilograms,
(c) Concorde – 185 tonnes,
(d) the liner *Queen Elizabeth II* – 67 000 tonnes,
(e) a Jumbo jet – 351·5 tonnes,
(f) a blue whale – 139 500 kilograms.

Ask your teacher what to do next.

Writing the time

This time can be written as 5.40 or 20 minutes to 6.

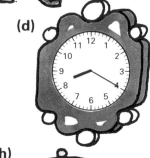

1 Write, in these two ways, the time shown on each clock:

(a)	(b)	(c)	(d)
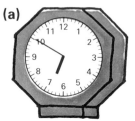	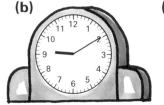		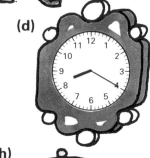

(e)	(f)	(g)	(h)
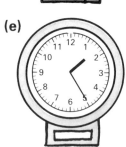	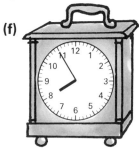		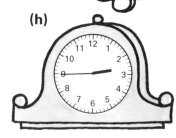

This digital time can be written as 8.35 or twenty-five to 9.

2 Write, in these two ways, the time shown on each digital display:

(a)	(b)	(c)	(d)

(e)	(f)	(g)	(h)

The time shown on each clock
is twenty-three minutes past 7.

3 Write one of the digital times given below to match each clock:

(a)	(b)	(c)	(d)

10:41 5:17 5:23 4:26 7:56 11:40

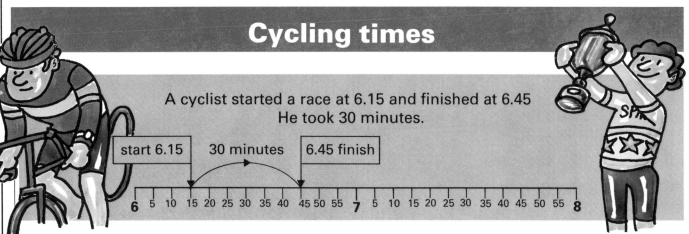

Cycling times

A cyclist started a race at 6.15 and finished at 6.45
He took 30 minutes.

| start 6.15 | 30 minutes | 6.45 finish |

6   5 10 15 20 25 30 35 40 45 50 55   7   5 10 15 20 25 30 35 40 45 50 55   8

1 Find the time taken by cyclists who started and finished a race at the times shown:

	(a)	(b)	(c)	(d)	(e)	(f)
start	6:10	6:25	6:05	7:20	7:30	7:05
finish	6:35	6:50	6:40	7:55	7:55	7:35

2 A road race was started at 6.00. The finishing times are shown.
How long did each cyclist take?

Amin	Brian	Colin	Don	Ellen	Frank
6:40	6:35	6:50	6:45	6:30	6:55

3 Six cyclists have to arrive at a checkpoint at 8.00. Their starting times are shown.
How many minutes does each cyclist have to reach the checkpoint?

7:15	7:20	7:25	7:10	7:05	7:30
Karen	Len	Mary	Nanji	Omar	Paul

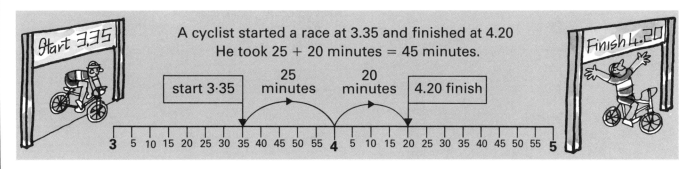

A cyclist started a race at 3.35 and finished at 4.20
He took 25 + 20 minutes = 45 minutes.

| start 3·35 | 25 minutes | 20 minutes | 4.20 finish |

3   5 10 15 20 25 30 35 40 45 50 55   4   5 10 15 20 25 30 35 40 45 50 55   5

4 Find the time taken by cyclists who started and finished at the times shown:

	(a)	(b)	(c)	(d)	(e)	(f)
start	3:25	3:50	3:15	3:45	3:40	3:35
finish	4:10	4:30	4:05	4:40	4:35	4:15

START
3.45

5 Find the time taken by this cyclist.

FINISH
4.25

Departures and arrivals

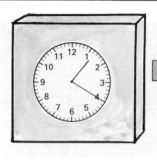

A bus left at 1.20 The journey took 25 minutes. When did it arrive?

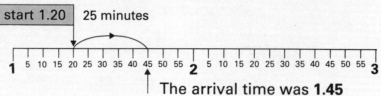

The arrival time was **1.45**

1 Find the arrival time of each bus.

	(a)	(b)	(c)	(d)	(e)	(f)	(g)
Leaves	1.00	1.30	1.05	2.25	2.35	2.45	2.05
Journey time	35 min	25 min	40 min	10 min	20 min	15 min	45 min

A school bus left at 1.40
It arrived at school after 45 minutes.
When did it arrive?

1.40 to 2.00 is 20 minutes.
There are 25 minutes more.
Arrival time is **2.25**

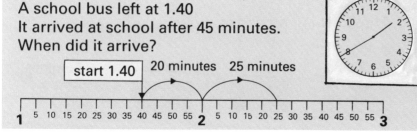

2 Find the arrival time of each bus.

	(a)	(b)	(c)	(d)	(e)	(f)	(g)
Departs	1.50	1.35	1.20	1.40	1.30	1.45	1.25
Journey time	45 min	50 min	55 min	35 min	40 min	45 min	50 min

A bus arrived at 12.25, after a journey of 35 minutes.
When did the bus start its journey?

Arrival time 12.25
Journey time 35 min
Starting time 11.50

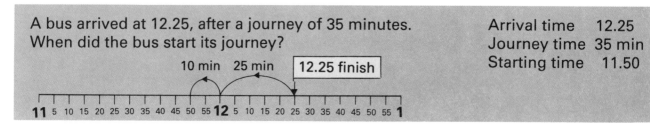

3 Find the starting time of each bus.

	(a)	(b)	(c)	(d)	(e)	(f)	(g)
Arrives	11.40	11.55	11.45	12.30	12.50	12.35	1.00
Journey time	30 min	50 min	35 min	25 min	40 min	20 min	45 min

4 Find the starting time of each bus.

	(a)	(b)	(c)	(d)	(e)	(f)	(g)
Arrives	12.30	12.40	12.10	12.25	12.20	12.15	12.35
Journey time	40 min	50 min	45 min	55 min	35 min	45 min	50 min

Parking times

1 Find the time **one hour after**:
(a) 4.30 pm   (b) 4.50 pm   (c) 5.25 pm   (d) 3.45 pm   (e) 12.55 pm

2 Find the time **two hours after**:
(a) 4.10 pm   (b) 4.45 pm   (c) 5.15 pm   (d) 3.35 pm   (e) 2.40 pm

3 Find the time **one hour earlier** than:
(a) 5.40 pm   (b) 5.15 pm   (c) 6.05 pm   (d) 4.35 pm   (e) 3.25 pm

4 Find the time **two hours earlier** than:
(a) 5.50 pm   (b) 4.40 pm   (c) 6.25 pm   (d) 3.20 pm   (e) 12.30 pm

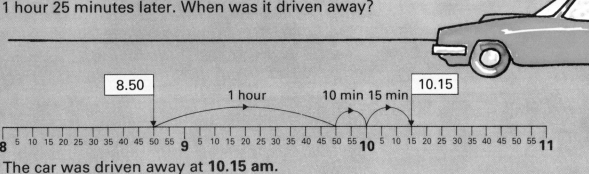

A car was parked at 8.50 am. It was driven away
1 hour 25 minutes later. When was it driven away?

The car was driven away at **10.15 am.**

5 Find the missing
times:

Car	Parked at	Parked for	Driven away at
Metro	8.40 am	1 hour 30 minutes	(a)
Escort	8.25 am	1 hour 45 minutes	(b)
Nova	9.35 am	1 hour 40 minutes	(c)
Rover	9.50 am	2 hours 35 minutes	(d)

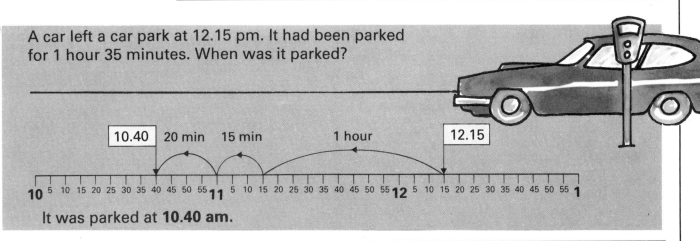

A car left a car park at 12.15 pm. It had been parked
for 1 hour 35 minutes. When was it parked?

It was parked at **10.40 am.**

6 Find when each
car was
parked.

Car	Parked at	Parked for	Left at
Sunny	(a)	1 hour 40 minutes	12.15 pm
Cherry	(b)	1 hour 55 minutes	12.10 pm
Corolla	(c)	2 hours 30 minutes	12.20 pm
Pony	(d)	2 hours 50 minutes	1.15 pm

Do Workbook Page 28.

W

Race times

In a car rally a Mini took 2 hours 25 minutes for one **leg** of a journey and 1 hour 17 minutes for a second leg. What was its total time for the two legs?

	h	min
1st leg	2	25
2nd leg	+ 1	17
Total time	3	42

1 Find the total time taken for the two legs by each car.

	Astra	Escort	Fiesta	Metro	Polo
1st leg	2 h 26 min	2 h 19 min	2 h 28 min	2 h 27 min	2 h 34 min
2nd leg	1 h 23 min	1 h 32 min	1 h 22 min	1 h 14 min	1 h 19 min

2 Change to hours and minutes:

(a) 90 min   (b) 75 min   (c) 86 min   (d) 100 min   (e) 102 min   (f) 110 min

The times taken by a motor-bike for two races were 47 minutes and 48 minutes. Find, in hours and minutes, the total time taken.

	h	min
1st race		47
2nd race	+	48
Total time	1	35
		95

3 Find, in hours and minutes, the total time taken for two races by each bike.

	Honda	Kawasaki	Suzuki	Triumph	Yamaha
1st race	49 min	46 min	49 min	45 min	48 min
2nd race	50 min	48 min	46 min	47 min	52 min

4 Find the total time taken for two legs by each car.

	Cavalier	Sierra	Jaguar	Montego	Rover
	h min				
1st leg	2 44	2 h 52 min	2 h 39 min	2 h 48 min	2 h 54 min
2nd leg	3 35	3 h 46 min	3 h 26 min	3 h 37 min	3 h 56 min
	6 19				
	79				

5 Change to minutes and seconds:

(a) 80 sec   (b) 72 sec   (c) 95 sec   (d) 65 sec   (e) 105 sec   (f) 115 sec

The times taken for two laps of a race were 39 seconds and 37 seconds. Find, in minutes and seconds, the total time taken.

	min	sec
1st lap		39
2nd lap	+	37
Total time	1	16
		76

6 Find, in minutes and seconds, the total time taken for the two laps shown.

	(a)	(b)	(c)	(d)	(e)	(f)
1st lap	42 sec	41 sec	1 min 43 sec	2 min 46 sec	3 min 52 sec	3 min 56 sec
2nd lap	36 sec	39 sec	1 min 24 sec	2 min 49 sec	3 min 53 sec	3 min 54 sec

Ask your teacher if you should do Graph Cards 12, 14, 16, 18, 20.

Co-ordinates

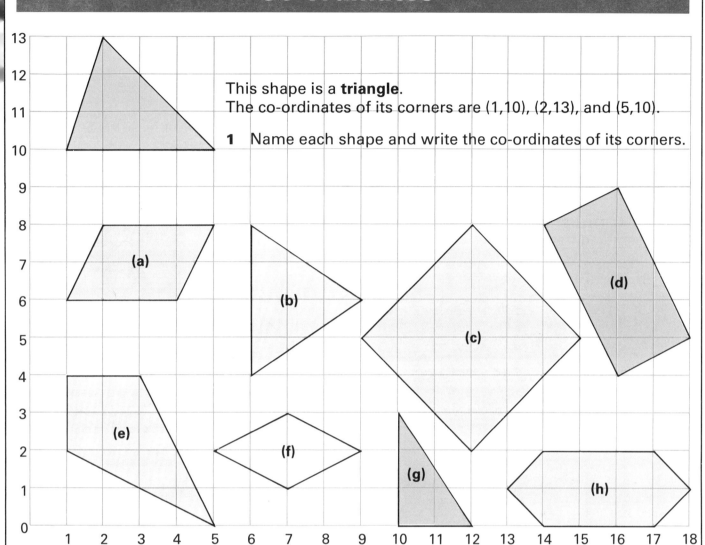

This shape is a **triangle**.
The co-ordinates of its corners are (1,10), (2,13), and (5,10).

1 Name each shape and write the co-ordinates of its corners.

(a) (b) (c) (d) (e) (f) (g) (h)

2 Do Workbook Page 13.

W

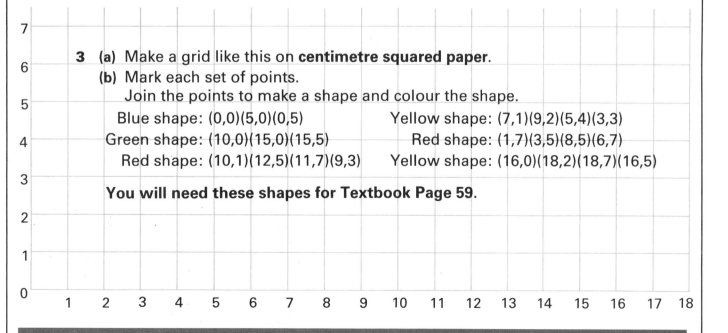

3 (a) Make a grid like this on **centimetre squared paper**.
(b) Mark each set of points.
    Join the points to make a shape and colour the shape.
    Blue shape: (0,0)(5,0)(0,5)   Yellow shape: (7,1)(9,2)(5,4)(3,3)
    Green shape: (10,0)(15,0)(15,5)   Red shape: (1,7)(3,5)(8,5)(6,7)
    Red shape: (10,1)(12,5)(11,7)(9,3)   Yellow shape: (16,0)(18,2)(18,7)(16,5)

You will need these shapes for Textbook Page 59.

Patterns

1 Here are two coloured patterns.
Name the different shapes used in each pattern.

(a)

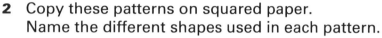

(b)

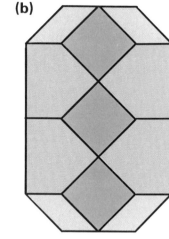

2 Copy these patterns on squared paper.
Name the different shapes used in each pattern.

(a)

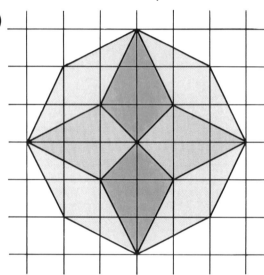

(b)

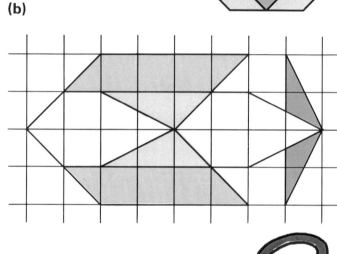

3 **(a)** Cut out the six shapes which you made for
Textbook Page 58, question **3**.

(b) Use one red shape and one yellow shape to make
this rhombus. Stick it in your jotter.

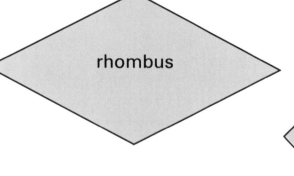

rhombus

hexagon

(c) Use the other four shapes to
make this hexagon.
Stick it in your jotter.

Tiling and enlarging

1   Here are some tilings. Name the shape used in each tiling.

(a) 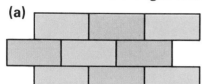   **(b)**    **(c)**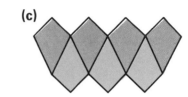

2   **You need sets of plastic or gummed shapes.**
   Fit the equilateral triangles together to find if they make a tiling.
   Repeat this for sets of the other shapes. List the shapes which tile.

equilateral   isosceles   rhombus   parallelogram   pentagon   hexagon
triangle   triangle

3   **Do Workbook Page 14.**   W

4   The photograph can be **enlarged** like this ——▶

   The photograph can be **reduced** like this ——▶

5   **Do Workbook Page 15.**   W

6   Using centimetre squared paper, draw these shapes, making each side
   (a) twice as long,   **(b) half** as long.

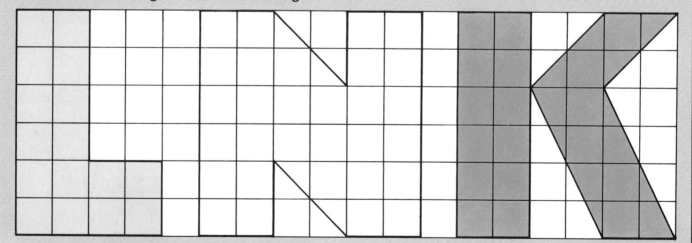

7   **Do Workbook Page 16.**   W

8   **Ask your teacher if you should do Shape Cards 2, 4, 6, 8, 10.**

Part 3 Acknowledgements

p 64. Farming Information Centre
p 66. Marc Henrie
p 71. P. Kemmett
p 82. National Exhibition Centre Ltd.

Part 3

Halves and quarters

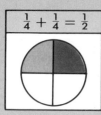

Remember

$\frac{1}{4} + \frac{1}{4} = \frac{1}{2}$

Find $2\frac{1}{4} + 3\frac{1}{4}$

$2\frac{1}{4} + 3\frac{1}{4}$

$= 5\frac{1}{2}$

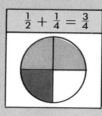

Remember

$\frac{1}{2} + \frac{1}{4} = \frac{3}{4}$

Find $1\frac{1}{2} + 1\frac{1}{4}$

$1\frac{1}{2} + 1\frac{1}{4}$

$= 2\frac{3}{4}$

1 Copy and complete:

(a) $7\frac{1}{4} + \frac{1}{4}$ (b) $5\frac{1}{4} + 1\frac{1}{4}$ (c) $\frac{1}{4} + 2\frac{1}{4}$ (d) $2\frac{1}{4} + 6\frac{1}{4}$ (e) $4\frac{1}{4} + 3$ (f) $10 + 1\frac{1}{4}$

(g) $3\frac{1}{2} + \frac{1}{4}$ (h) $\frac{1}{2} + 4\frac{1}{4}$ (i) $2\frac{1}{2} + 5\frac{1}{4}$ (j) $7\frac{1}{4} + \frac{1}{2}$ (k) $1\frac{1}{4} + 5\frac{1}{2}$ (l) $\frac{1}{4} + 4\frac{1}{2}$

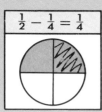

Remember

$\frac{1}{2} - \frac{1}{4} = \frac{1}{4}$

Find $4\frac{1}{2} - 1\frac{1}{4}$

$4\frac{1}{2} - 1\frac{1}{4}$

$= 3\frac{1}{4}$

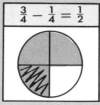

Remember

$\frac{3}{4} - \frac{1}{4} = \frac{1}{2}$

Find $3\frac{3}{4} - 2\frac{1}{4}$

$3\frac{3}{4} - 2\frac{1}{4}$

$= 1\frac{1}{2}$

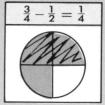

Remember

$\frac{3}{4} - \frac{1}{2} = \frac{1}{4}$

Find $5\frac{3}{4} - 3\frac{1}{2}$

$5\frac{3}{4} - 3\frac{1}{2}$

$= 2\frac{1}{4}$

2 Copy and complete:

(a) $3\frac{1}{2} - \frac{1}{4}$ (b) $6\frac{1}{2} - 2\frac{1}{4}$ (c) $4\frac{1}{2} - 4\frac{1}{4}$ (d) $7\frac{1}{2} - 6\frac{1}{4}$ (e) $3\frac{3}{4} - \frac{1}{4}$ (f) $5\frac{3}{4} - 2\frac{1}{4}$

(g) $4\frac{3}{4} - 4\frac{1}{4}$ (h) $5\frac{3}{4} - \frac{1}{2}$ (i) $8\frac{3}{4} - 6\frac{1}{2}$ (j) $3\frac{3}{4} - 3\frac{1}{2}$ (k) $7\frac{1}{2} - 1\frac{1}{4}$ (l) $9\frac{3}{4} - 8\frac{1}{2}$

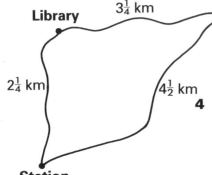

Library · $3\frac{1}{4}$ km · School

$2\frac{1}{4}$ km · $4\frac{1}{2}$ km

Station

3 How far is it from
(a) the station to the school via the library,
(b) the station to the library via the school,
(c) the school to the library via the station?

4 How much further is it from
(a) the station to the school **than** the station to the library,
(b) the school to the station **than** the school to the library,
(c) the library to the school **than** the library to the station?

5 Tom spent $1\frac{1}{4}$ hours cleaning the car and $2\frac{1}{2}$ hours cleaning the caravan.
(a) How long was this altogether?
(b) How much longer did he spend cleaning the caravan than the car?

6 (a) What is the total weight of the flour and the sugar?
(b) What is the weight of the sugar?

FLOUR $1\frac{1}{2}$ kg · SUGAR

7 A painter mixed $3\frac{1}{4}$ litres of white paint with $\frac{1}{2}$ litre of green paint.
(a) How much paint is this altogether?
(b) If $2\frac{1}{2}$ litres of the paint are used, how much is left?

PAINT

Halves and quarters

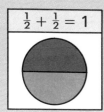

$\frac{1}{2} + \frac{1}{2} = 1$

Find $3\frac{1}{2} + 2\frac{1}{2}$

$3\frac{1}{2} + 2\frac{1}{2}$

$= 6$

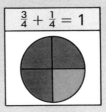

$\frac{3}{4} + \frac{1}{4} = 1$

Find $4\frac{3}{4} + 2\frac{1}{4}$

$4\frac{3}{4} + 2\frac{1}{4}$

$= 7$

1 Copy and complete:

(a) $1\frac{1}{2} + 6\frac{1}{2}$ (b) $3\frac{1}{4} + 1\frac{3}{4}$ (c) $2\frac{3}{4} + 5\frac{1}{4}$ (d) $\frac{1}{2} + 4\frac{1}{2}$ (e) $7\frac{1}{4} + \frac{3}{4}$ (f) $5\frac{3}{4} + 4\frac{1}{4}$

2

	Moira	Linda
Wednesday	$2\frac{1}{2}$	$1\frac{1}{4}$
Saturday	$3\frac{1}{2}$	$5\frac{3}{4}$

The table shows the hours worked by Moira and Linda.

(a) Who worked more hours altogether?

(b) How many more hours did Linda work than Moira on Saturday?

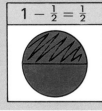

$1 - \frac{1}{2} = \frac{1}{2}$

Find $6 - \frac{1}{2}$

$6 - \frac{1}{2}$

$= 5\frac{1}{2}$

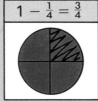

$1 - \frac{1}{4} = \frac{3}{4}$

Find $6 - \frac{1}{4}$

$6 - \frac{1}{4}$

$= 5\frac{3}{4}$

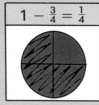

$1 - \frac{3}{4} = \frac{1}{4}$

Find $6 - \frac{3}{4}$

$6 - \frac{3}{4}$

$= 5\frac{1}{4}$

3 Copy and complete:

(a) $5 - \frac{1}{2}$ (b) $6 - \frac{1}{4}$ (c) $3 - \frac{3}{4}$ (d) $10 - \frac{1}{4}$ (e) $15 - \frac{1}{2}$ (f) $24 - \frac{1}{4}$

4 Mr Fixit bought a 4 m length of guttering and a 2 m length of pipe.

(a) He cut $\frac{1}{2}$ m off the guttering. What length was left?

(b) He cut $\frac{1}{4}$ m off the pipe. What length was left?

$1\frac{1}{4}$ litres of orange juice is poured from a 4 litre container. How much is left?

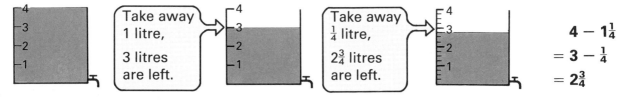

Take away 1 litre, 3 litres are left.

Take away $\frac{1}{4}$ litre, $2\frac{3}{4}$ litres are left.

$4 - 1\frac{1}{4}$

$= 3 - \frac{1}{4}$

$= 2\frac{3}{4}$

5 Copy and complete:

(a) $6 - 3\frac{1}{2}$ (b) $4 - 1\frac{3}{4}$ (c) $5 - 2\frac{1}{4}$ (d) $5 - 4\frac{1}{2}$ (e) $8 - 7\frac{1}{4}$ (f) $10 - 5\frac{3}{4}$

(g) $3 - 1\frac{1}{4}$ (h) $9 - 7\frac{1}{2}$ (i) $6 - 5\frac{3}{4}$ (j) $7 - 5\frac{1}{2}$ (k) $6 - 1\frac{1}{4}$ (l) $4 - 3\frac{3}{4}$

6 Mrs Ford bought a 5 litre can of oil.

(a) She used $3\frac{1}{4}$ litres for her car. How much was left in the can?

(b) Later she used another $\frac{1}{2}$ litre of oil. How much was **then** left in the can?

Ask your teacher what to do next.

Hotel Decima Lido

> **3·14**
> **×2**
> **6·28**
>
> 2 times 4 hundredths is 8 hundredths.
> 2 times 1 tenth is 2 tenths.
> 2 times 3 units is 6 units.

1 (a) 2·13 (b) 1·02 (c) 0·41 (d) 0·03 (e) 3·32 (f) 3·21 (g) 2·11
      ×3   ×4   ×2   ×2   ×3   ×4   ×5

2 Copy and complete this example.

> **1·46**
> **×3**
> **8**
> **1**
>
> 3 times 6 hundredths is 18 hundredths.
> 18 hundredths is 1 tenth and 8 hundredths.

3 (a) 2·45 (b) 1·56 (c) 1·34 (d) 0·24 (e) 2·18 (f) 1·24 (g) 2·14
      ×3   ×2   ×5   ×4   ×6   ×7   ×8

4 (a) 0·76 × 2 (b) 3 × 0·47 (c) 1·29 × 4 (d) 1·26 × 5 (e) 7 × 1·65 (f) 1·19 × 9

5 Find the product of (a) 2·61 and 7, (b) 8 and 1·55, (c) 3·09 and 6, (d) 9 and 2·23

6 A guest at Hotel Decima Lido wished to exchange £9 for U.S. dollars.
She was given 1·46 dollars for each £1.
How many dollars did she get for her £9?

7 (a) What did it cost a guest for 7 nights in the hotel at £30·25 per night?
(b) He also had 4 lunches at £4·75 each and 6 dinners
at £12·25 each. What was the **total** cost of all these meals?

8 Eight beach umbrellas were broken in a storm.
How much would it cost to replace them at £14·23 each?

9 Seven new chairs costing £72·15 each were bought for
the dining room. What did they cost altogether?

10 The wall of a bedroom is 2·45 m high.
If 7 strips of wallpaper are required to
cover the wall, what total length of
wallpaper is needed?

11 There are 10 trees in a straight line
along one side of the hotel. The trees
are about 4·25 m apart. About how far
is it from the first to the last tree?

Bales and nails

1 **Use a calculator.** Copy and complete:

(a) 0·03   ×10   (b) 0·46   ×10   (c) 3·14   ×10   (d) 2·48   ×10   (e) 4·87   ×10   (f) 1·09   ×10   (g) 5·61   ×10

2·65
×10
26·5

To multiply by 10, move each digit **one** place to the left.

2 Do these mentally and write your answers.

(a) 10 × 1·04   (b) 5·73 × 10   (c) 10 × 3·56   (d) 4·98 × 10   (e) 10 × 12·34   (f) 2·08 × 10

3 A bale of straw is about 1·25 m long. Ten bales are placed end to end in a straight line.
About how long is the line of bales?

4 The average weight of a bag of grain is 50·25 kg. Find the weight of 10 bags.

5 How much would it cost a farmer to pay 10 helpers £16·75 each?

6 **Use a calculator.** Copy and complete:

(a) 0·68   ×100   (b) 0·53   ×100   (c) 1·06   ×100   (d) 4·89   ×100   (e) 3·02   ×100   (f) 2·56   ×100   (g) 5·2   ×100

1·47
×100
147·

To multiply by 100, move each digit **two** places to the left.

7 Do these mentally and write your answers.

(a) 100 × 0·92   (b) 0·46 × 100   (c) 100 × 3·14   (d) 5·67 × 100   (e) 100 × 9·05

8 A worker in a nail factory is paid £3·86 per hour.
What does she earn for 100 hours work?

9 About what length of wire is needed to make 100 wire nails each 9·15 cm long?
Give your answer in metres and centimetres.

10 One nail weighs about 8·9 g. What is the total weight of 100 of these nails?

Joiner Bill

You can find 6·39 ÷ 3 like this:

Share the 6 units ⟶ 6 ÷ 3 = 2

$$\begin{array}{r} 2 \\ 3\overline{\smash{)}6{\cdot}3\,9} \end{array}$$

Share the 3 tenths ⟶ 3 ÷ 3 = 1

$$\begin{array}{r} 2{\cdot}1 \\ 3\overline{\smash{)}6{\cdot}3\,9} \end{array}$$

Share the 9 hundredths ⟶ 9 ÷ 3 = 3

$$\begin{array}{r} 2{\cdot}1\,3 \\ 3\overline{\smash{)}6{\cdot}3\,9} \end{array}$$

1 (a) $2\overline{)4{\cdot}28}$ (b) $2\overline{)8{\cdot}46}$ (c) $3\overline{)3{\cdot}66}$ (d) $4\overline{)0{\cdot}48}$ (e) $2\overline{)6{\cdot}02}$ (f) $2\overline{)0{\cdot}04}$

2 (a) 0·69 ÷ 3 (b) 9·36 ÷ 3 (c) 8·02 ÷ 2 (d) 0·46 ÷ 2 (e) 4·84 ÷ 4

You can find 2·16 ÷ 4 like this:

Share the 2 units ⟶ 2 ÷ 4 = 0 remainder 2

$$\begin{array}{r} 0{\cdot} \\ 4\overline{\smash{)}2{\cdot}^{2}1\,6} \end{array}$$

Share the 21 tenths ⟶ 21 ÷ 4 = 5 remainder 1

$$\begin{array}{r} 0{\cdot}\,5 \\ 4\overline{\smash{)}2{\cdot}^{2}1^{1}6} \end{array}$$

Share the 16 hundredths ⟶ 16 ÷ 4 = 4

$$\begin{array}{r} 0{\cdot}\,5\,4 \\ 4\overline{\smash{)}2{\cdot}^{2}1^{1}6} \end{array}$$

3 (a) $3\overline{)2{\cdot}34}$ (b) $4\overline{)0{\cdot}28}$ (c) $6\overline{)5{\cdot}04}$ (d) $8\overline{)8{\cdot}64}$ (e) $7\overline{)9{\cdot}45}$ (f) $5\overline{)2{\cdot}05}$

4 (a) 1·32 ÷ 4 (b) 4·15 ÷ 5 (c) 3·99 ÷ 7 (d) 8·24 ÷ 8 (e) 7·38 ÷ 6 (f) 9·25 ÷ 5

5 (a) 8·19 ÷ 9 (b) 12·46 ÷ 7 (c) 27·00 ÷ 4 (d) 7·35 ÷ 7 (e) 1·08 ÷ 9 (f) 18·00 ÷ 8

6 Find: (a) $\frac{1}{3}$ of 26·88 (b) $\frac{1}{6}$ of 21·30 (c) $\frac{1}{8}$ of 19·44 (d) $\frac{1}{4}$ of 9·00 (e) $\frac{1}{2}$ of 7·60

7 Bill the joiner cuts a plank of wood 6·45 m long into 5 parts of equal length. What length is each part?

8 Bill earned £178·75 for a five-day week. Find his average **daily** earnings.

9 Eight boxes of brass screws cost Bill £16·40. What is the price of 1 box of screws?

10 Bill paid a cleaner £29 altogether for sweeping out his workshop on 4 days. What was the cleaner's **average daily payment?**

Pets and games

1 **Use a calculator.** Copy and complete:

(a) $10\overline{)16\cdot2}$ (b) $10\overline{)13\cdot4}$ (c) $10\overline{)2\cdot5}$ (d) $10\overline{)1\cdot9}$ (e) $10\overline{)21\cdot6}$ (f) $10\overline{)17\cdot2}$

$$10\overline{)2\ 4\cdot3}^{\ 2\cdot4\ 3}$$ To divide by 10, move each digit **one** place to the right.

2 Do these mentally and write your answers.

(a) $30\cdot2 \div 10$ (b) $86\cdot3 \div 10$ (c) $28\cdot6 \div 10$ (d) $41\cdot5 \div 10$ (e) $9\cdot8 \div 10$ (f) $0\cdot7 \div 10$

3 A setter's 10 pups weigh 13·4 kg altogether. What is the average weight of one pup?

4 Mr Barker owned the pups. He paid £14·30 one week for dog food. What was the average cost of dog food for **one** pup?

5 When the pups grew up their total weight was 278·5 kg. What was their new average weight?

6 **Use a calculator.** Copy and complete:

(a) $100\overline{)143}$ (b) $100\overline{)286}$ (c) $100\overline{)317}$ (d) $100\overline{)748}$ (e) $100\overline{)12}$ (f) $100\overline{)9}$

$$100\overline{)4\ 1\ 2\cdot}^{\ 4\cdot1\ 2}$$ To divide by 100, move each digit **two** places to the right.

7 Do these mentally and write your answers.

(a) $123 \div 100$ (b) $876 \div 100$ (c) $108 \div 100$ (d) $350 \div 100$ (e) $42 \div 100$ (f) $8 \div 100$

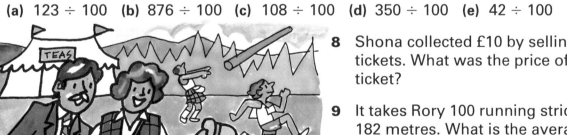

8 Shona collected £10 by selling 100 raffle tickets. What was the price of each raffle ticket?

9 It takes Rory 100 running strides to cover 182 metres. What is the average length in metres of **one** stride?

10 A hundred spectators spent £385 altogether in the refreshment tent. What was the average amount spent by each spectator?

11 Altogether 47 boys and 53 girls drank 25 litres of coke. Find the average amount of coke drunk by each child.

Ask your teacher if you should do Number Cards 41, 43, 45, 47, 49.

Alan buys these 3 articles from the shop. ⟶
The total cost is 59p + £2·48 + £1·13

The total can be worked out using a calculator.

Enter 59p as ▮ 0.59

Add £2·48 by pressing the keys ➕ 2 • 4 8

Add £1·13 by pressing ➕ 1 • 1 3 and then ⟰ to give ▮ 4.2

The total cost is £4·20

1   Find the total cost of:
   (a) a calculator, a diary, and a pen and pencil set,
   (b) a DAB glue stick, a packet of felt pens, and SWISH writing paper and envelopes,
   (c) an eraser, a ruler, and a pencil,
   (d) a calculator, an eraser, and a packet of felt pens,
   (e) a Wondapen, a packet of felt pens, and a packet of coloured pencils.

2   These are receipts from the shop. The first one shows the
   change given. Use a calculator to find the change for each
   of the other receipts.

| | (a) | (b) | (c) |

```
DRAW WRITE LTD

STATIONERY    2.35
AMT. TENDERED 5.00
CHANGE        2.65
```

```
DRAW WRITE LTD

STATIONERY    6.18
AMT. TENDERED 10.00
CHANGE
```

```
DRAW WRITE LTD

STATIONERY    2.85
AMT. TENDERED 5.00
CHANGE
```

```
DRAW WRITE LTD

STATIONERY    18.54
AMT. TENDERED 20.00
CHANGE
```

3   Alice bought SWISH writing paper and envelopes.
   Her brother Bill bought a packet of coloured pencils.
   (a) How much did Alice and Bill pay altogether?
   (b) Find the **difference** in the amounts they paid.

Alan buys 12 rulers from the shop. The total cost is 26p ✕ 12.

The cost can be worked out using a calculator.

Enter 26p as   `0.26`

Multiply by 12 by pressing ✕ 1 2 = to give   `3.12`

The total cost is £3·12

1 Find the cost of:
   (a) 18 pencils,   **(b)** 26 packets of felt pens,   **(c)** 15 pen and pencil sets,
   (d) 20 diaries,   **(e)** 35 glue sticks and 35 rulers.

2 What is the change from £10 after buying   **(a)** 13 erasers,   **(b)** two dozen pencils?

3 The total of each of these receipts is missing.
   Multiply to find each total.

(a)
```
DRAW WRITE LTD

P/P SET    5.76
P/P SET    5.76
P/P SET    5.76
P/P SET    5.76
P/P SET    5.76
TOTAL
```

(b)
```
DRAW WRITE LTD

CALCTR    6.18
CALCTR    6.18
CALCTR    6.18
CALCTR    6.18
CALCTR    6.18
CALCTR    6.18
CALCTR    6.18
CALCTR    6.18
TOTAL
```

4 John bought 8 identical items from the shop. The total bill was £9·04.
   Which item did he buy?

```
TOTAL    9.04
```

```
TOTAL
AMT. TENDERED 20.00
CHANGE        4.32
```

5 **(a)** Jane received £4·32 change from £20.
      How much did she spend?
   (b) She spent this amount on seven identical items from the shop. Which item did she buy?

6 If you had £20 to spend in this shop, what would you buy?
   Write out your bill including total and change.

Ask your teacher what to do next.

Fractions greater than 1

The whole tart has been cut into 4 quarters.

$$\frac{4}{4} = 1$$

There are 12 quarter tarts on the tray. They make 3 whole tarts.

$$\frac{12}{4} = 3$$

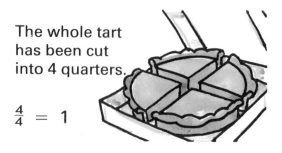

1 Copy and complete what is shown by each picture.

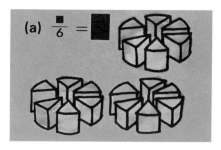

(a) $\frac{\blacksquare}{6} = \blacksquare$

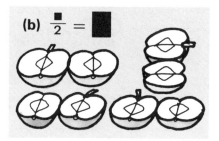

(b) $\frac{\blacksquare}{2} = \blacksquare$

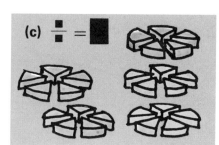

(c) $\frac{\blacksquare}{\blacksquare} = \blacksquare$

There are 11 quarter cakes on the table. They make $2\frac{3}{4}$ cakes.

$$\frac{11}{4} = 2\frac{3}{4}$$

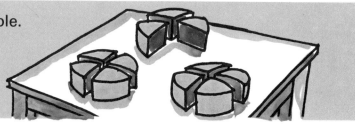

2 Copy and complete what is shown by each picture.

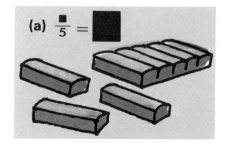

(a) $\frac{\blacksquare}{5} = \blacksquare$

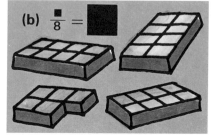

(b) $\frac{\blacksquare}{8} = \blacksquare$

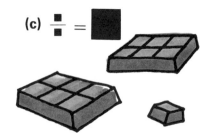

(c) $\frac{\blacksquare}{\blacksquare} = \blacksquare$

(d) $\frac{\blacksquare}{\blacksquare} = \blacksquare$ Each piece is $\frac{1}{4}$ of a cake.

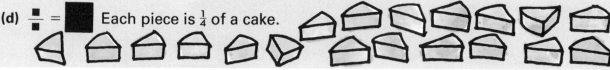

W **3** Do Workbook Page 29.

To change 13 fifths to a mixed number
divide 13 by 5 to give 2 wholes and 3 fifths $\frac{13}{5} = 2\frac{3}{5}$

4 Write each fraction as a mixed number:

(a) $\frac{7}{6}$ (b) $\frac{17}{10}$ (c) $\frac{13}{8}$ (d) $\frac{21}{5}$ (e) $\frac{25}{4}$ (f) $\frac{16}{3}$

(g) $\frac{7}{2}$ (h) $\frac{23}{6}$ (i) $\frac{14}{5}$ (j) $\frac{73}{10}$ (k) $\frac{67}{8}$ (l) $\frac{29}{3}$

Simplifying fractions

A fraction may be simplified by dividing **numerator and denominator** by the same number.

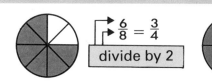 $\frac{6}{8} = \frac{3}{4}$ divide by 2

 $\frac{5}{10} = \frac{1}{2}$ divide by 5

1 Simplify: **(a)** $\frac{2}{8}$ **(b)** $\frac{8}{10}$ **(c)** $\frac{4}{6}$ **(d)** $\frac{15}{20}$ **(e)** $\frac{9}{12}$ **(f)** $\frac{10}{16}$ **(g)** $\frac{10}{25}$ **(h)** $\frac{3}{30}$ **(i)** $\frac{6}{15}$

$3\frac{6}{10} = 3\frac{3}{5}$

2 Simplify: **(a)** $3\frac{2}{6}$ **(b)** $1\frac{3}{12}$ **(c)** $5\frac{6}{10}$ **(d)** $4\frac{9}{15}$ **(e)** $2\frac{20}{25}$ **(f)** $1\frac{5}{20}$

Sometimes to simplify a fraction we divide numerator and denominator **more than once**.

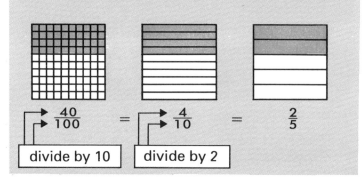

$\frac{40}{100}$ = $\frac{4}{10}$ = $\frac{2}{5}$

divide by 10   divide by 2

3 Simplify:

(a) $\frac{20}{80}$ **(b)** $\frac{80}{100}$ **(c)** $\frac{50}{200}$ **(d)** $\frac{25}{50}$

(e) $\frac{24}{60}$ **(f)** $\frac{12}{72}$ **(g)** $\frac{25}{100}$ **(h)** $\frac{16}{48}$

(i) $\frac{24}{36}$ **(j)** $\frac{50}{75}$ **(k)** $4\frac{40}{80}$ **(l)** $2\frac{75}{100}$

(m) $3\frac{20}{100}$ **(n)** $1\frac{40}{60}$ **(o)** $1\frac{18}{24}$ **(p)** $5\frac{36}{60}$

4 In these examples, simplify each answer.

(a) $\frac{3}{8} + \frac{1}{8}$ **(b)** $\frac{9}{10} - \frac{3}{10}$ **(c)** $\frac{5}{6} - \frac{1}{6}$ **(d)** $\frac{7}{20} + \frac{3}{20}$ **(e)** $\frac{18}{25} - \frac{3}{25}$ **(f)** $\frac{17}{100} + \frac{23}{100}$

(g) $1\frac{3}{10} + 2\frac{1}{10}$ **(h)** $3\frac{5}{8} - 1\frac{1}{8}$ **(i)** $4\frac{7}{10} - \frac{1}{10}$ **(j)** $\frac{9}{20} + 1\frac{3}{20}$ **(k)** $1\frac{1}{12} + 2\frac{7}{12}$ **(l)** $4\frac{7}{16} - 1\frac{3}{16}$

$\frac{26}{12} = \frac{13}{6} = 2\frac{1}{6}$

5 Simplify each fraction and write it as a mixed number.

(a) $\frac{14}{4}$ **(b)** $\frac{25}{10}$ **(c)** $\frac{10}{8}$ **(d)** $\frac{22}{12}$ **(e)** $\frac{44}{20}$ **(f)** $\frac{120}{50}$ **(g)** $\frac{35}{15}$

$4\frac{3}{8} + 2\frac{7}{8}$

$= 6\frac{10}{8}$

$= 6\frac{5}{4}$ ← $\frac{5}{4}$ is $1\frac{1}{4}$

$= 7\frac{1}{4}$ 6 and $1\frac{1}{4}$ is $7\frac{1}{4}$

6 **(a)** $\frac{2}{3} + \frac{2}{3}$ **(b)** $\frac{4}{5} + \frac{3}{5}$ **(c)** $\frac{9}{15} + \frac{8}{15}$

(d) $3\frac{3}{5} + \frac{3}{5}$ **(e)** $\frac{2}{3} + 2\frac{1}{3}$ **(f)** $2\frac{3}{10} + 1\frac{7}{10}$

(g) $\frac{5}{8} + \frac{7}{8}$ **(h)** $1\frac{5}{6} + \frac{5}{6}$ **(i)** $3\frac{7}{10} + 2\frac{9}{10}$

(j) $1\frac{19}{20} + 2\frac{6}{20}$ **(k)** $\frac{5}{12} + 2\frac{11}{12}$ **(l)** $1\frac{15}{16} + 3\frac{5}{16}$

7 Jim worked in his garden for $2\frac{3}{4}$ hours in the afternoon and $1\frac{3}{4}$ hours in the evening. How long did he work altogether?

What fraction is it?

There are 13 pens.
6 of the pens are green.
The fraction of pens which are green is $\frac{6}{13}$.

1 What fraction of the pens are
  (a) red,   **(b)** yellow?

2 There are 25 flowers in a vase. 13 flowers are tulips and 12 are daffodils.
What fraction of the flowers are **(a)** tulips,   **(b)** daffodils?

3 Measure in centimetres the lengths of
(a) the whole line,   **(b)** the green part,   **(c)** the red part,   **(d)** the blue part.

4 What fraction of the whole line is **(a)** green,   **(b)** red,   **(c)** blue?

5 In a class of 25 children, 17 had calculators.
What fraction of the class **(a)** had a calculator,   **(b)** did **not** have a calculator?

John delivered 60 Sunday newspapers.
18 of the papers were the *Sunday Herald*.

The fraction of John's papers which were
the *Sunday Herald* was $\frac{18}{60} = \frac{3}{10}$

6 Of the 200 pages in a book, 25 pages are photographs and 40 pages are drawings.
What fraction of the pages are **(a)** photographs,   **(b)** drawings?

7 In September there was sunshine on only 6 days.
What fraction of the days in September had **no** sunshine?

8 Out of her £1 pocket money, Susan spent 40p.
What fraction of her pocket money had she left?

9 A school football team won 10 games, lost 9 games, and drew 5 games.
(a) How many games were played?
(b) What fraction of the games played were lost?

Lynn's records

Pop
Rock
Jazz

0   20   40   60   80
Number of records

10 Lynn paid £4 to travel to a Pop concert, £12 for the ticket,
£3 for a souvenir programme, and £1 for a snack.
What fraction of the total money was spent on the ticket?

11 The graph shows the types of records in Lynn's collection.
What fraction of her records are
(a) Pop,   **(b)** Rock,   **(c)** Jazz?

Ask your teacher what to do next.

Distances and rainfall

This **spike graph** shows the distance, **to the nearest 10 km**, from Glasgow to some other towns and cities.

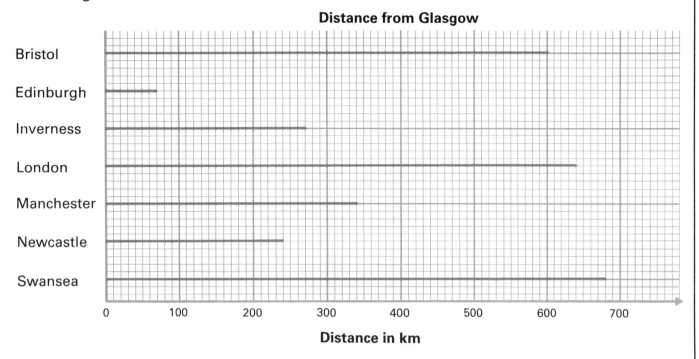

Distance from Glasgow

Distance in km

1 Which of these places is **(a)** furthest from Glasgow, **(b)** nearest to Glasgow?

2 What does each small interval on the distance axis represent?

3 How far is **each** of these seven places from Glasgow?

This **spike graph** shows the monthly rainfall in the Lake District for one year. The rain was collected and measured **to the nearest cm**.

4 Which month had
(a) the highest rainfall,
(b) the lowest rainfall?

5 Which month had the same rainfall as
(a) February,
(b) March?

6 Which months had a rainfall of more than 1 cm per day?

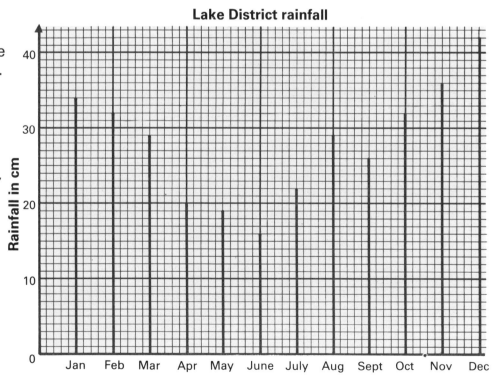

Lake District rainfall

Do Workbook Pages 30, 31, and 32.

W

Walking and jogging

A boy walks at a steady pace. The graph shows the distances he walks in certain times.

The dotted lines show that he walks 4 km in 1 hour.

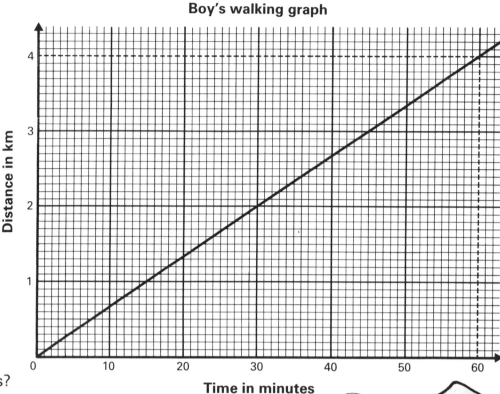

Boy's walking graph

1 What does each small interval represent on the time axis?

2 How many **metres** does each small interval represent on the distance axis?

3 How far does the boy walk in
(a) 30 minutes, (b) 15 minutes, (c) $\frac{3}{4}$ hour?

4 How long does the boy take to walk
(a) $3\frac{1}{2}$ km, (b) 1·5 km, (c) 2 km 500 m?

You need centimetre squared paper.

5 A girl jogs at a steady pace.
She travels 8 km in an hour.
Draw her straight-line jogging graph.
Mark the time axis to 90 minutes and the distance axis to 12 km.

6 Use your graph to find how long she takes to jog
(a) 4 km, (b) 12 km.

7 Use your graph to find how far she jogs in
(a) 45 minutes, (b) $1\frac{1}{4}$ hours.

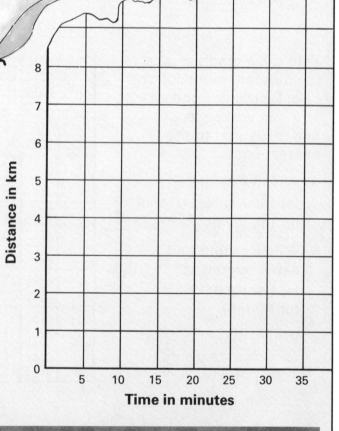

Ask your teacher if you should do Graph Cards 51, 53, 55, 57, 59.

24-hour times

Some clocks and watches show 24-hour times. Roy's watch is a 24-hour digital watch.

Remember: There are 24 hours in 1 day.

At 9 am Roy's watch shows ▶ **09:00**
This time is written 09.00

At 4 pm Roy's watch shows ▶ **16:00**
This time is written 16.00

Look at these times:	12-hour time	11 am	12 noon	1 pm	2 pm
	24-hour time	11.00	12.00	13.00	14.00

1 Write each time as a 24-hour time.

(a) 7 am   (b) 3 pm   (c) 5 pm   (d) 2 am   (e) 4 pm   (f) 11 pm
(g) 9 pm   (h) 6 am   (i) 3 am   (j) 10 am   (k) 8 pm   (l) 1 am

2 Write each time as a 12-hour time, using am or pm.

(a) 04.00   (b) 18.00   (c) 09.00   (d) 22.00   (e) 19.00   (f) 01.00
(g) 20.00   (h) 12.00   (i) 10.00   (j) 05.00   (k) 08.00   (l) 17.00

Kick-off 7.45 pm
___
Bestime United
v
Midwatch
___
Cup – 3rd round

This time is 19.45 as a 24-hour time.

Remember: Four figures are always used for 24-hour times.

19.45
hours ⟨⇦ ⇨⟩ minutes

Nineteen forty-five.

BESTIME UNITED

3 Change each time to a 24-hour time.

(a) Coach leaves 9.30 am
(b) Film starts 6.20 pm
(c) Next collection 8.15 am
(d) Closes at 8.45 pm

13:50   is written as **1.50 pm** or **ten minutes to two** in the afternoon.

4 Change each time to a 12-hour time, using am or pm.

(a)    (b)    (c)    (d)

5 Find each missing time.

24-hour time	09.15	17.55	(b)	(c)	23.45	(e)	01.10	21.05	03.50
12-hour time	9.15 am	(a)	8.25 pm	4.05 am	(d)	10.20 pm	(f)	(g)	(h)

Programme and train times

SATELLITE TV   Space TV

5.00   Newstime
5.10   The Animal Show
5.35   Quickquiz
6.00   Evening News
6.35   Reporting Britain
7.00   Stars from Europe
7.35   Errol's Way
8.05   Women's World
9.00   News at Nine
9.25   Space Stories
10.15 Sporting Chance

These are **evening** programme times.

1   Which programme starts at
(a) 17.00   (b) 17.10   (c) 21.00   (d) 21.25?

2   Which programme is on at
(a) 17.20   (b) 21.30   (c) 19.10   (d) 17.50?

3   Some video-recorders use a 24-hour clock.
What starting time will you set to record
(a) Quickquiz,   (b) Sporting Chance,   (c) Errol's Way,
(d) Women's World?

4   Train times are usually written as 24-hour times with **no dot** ⟶ 16.15 becomes **1615**

1 Aberdeen 11 50   2 Edinburgh 11 15   3 Glasgow 12 10   4 Perth 13 05   5 Stirling 1240

Which train leaves at
(a) quarter past eleven,   (b) five past one,
(c) ten to 12,   (d) twenty to 1?

5   The station master arrived at the station at 11.35
(a) Was he in time to see the Aberdeen train leave?
(b) How many minutes earlier had the Edinburgh train left?
(c) How long did he wait for the Glasgow train to leave?

This is a timetable for trains from Aberdeen to Glasgow.
Train **A** leaves Aberdeen at 9.05 am and arrives in Glasgow at 11.50 am.

	Train A	Train B	Train C	Train D	Train E
Aberdeen	0905	1105	1325	1505	1705
Dundee	1025	1225	1447	1625	1825
Perth	1047	1247	1509	1647	1847
Stirling	1119	1319	1542	1719	1919
Glasgow	1150	1350	1619	1750	1950

6   Which trains (a) leave Aberdeen after noon,   (b) arrive in Glasgow before 2 pm?

7   Which train (a) leaves Dundee at twenty-five past four,
(b) arrives in Glasgow at ten to eight?

8   To be in Perth by 4 pm, which is the latest train you could take from Aberdeen?

9   If you arrived at Dundee station at ten past four in the afternoon and took the next Glasgow train, when would you arrive in Glasgow?

Ask your teacher if you should do Workbook Page 37.

Journeys

The screen shows plane **departure** times from London.

The flight to Aberdeen takes 1 hour 20 minutes. When will the plane arrive in Aberdeen?

	h	min
Departure	11	45
Journey time	+1	20
	13	05
		65

The plane will arrive in Aberdeen at **5 past 1** in the afternoon.

Departures to

Aberdeen	1145
Inverness	1050
Dublin	1155
Orkney	1040
Shetland	1115

1 Find the **arrival** time for each journey.
(a) 1 hour 10 minutes to Dublin
(b) 3 hours 25 minutes to Shetland
(c) 2 hours 30 minutes to Orkney
(d) 1 hour 55 minutes to Inverness

Arrivals from

Dundee	1310
Edinburgh	1250
Stornoway	1330
Jersey	1335
Benbecula	1305

The screen shows plane arrival times at London Airport.

The flight from Dundee took 2 hours 40 minutes. When did the plane leave Dundee?

	h	min
Arrival	13^{12}	10^{60}
Flight time	−2	40
	10	30

The plane left Dundee at **10.30 am**.

2 Find the departure time for each journey.
(a) 1 hour 15 minutes from Edinburgh
(b) 2 hours 45 minutes from Stornoway
(c) 3 hours 10 minutes from Benbecula
(d) 50 minutes from Jersey

A bus left Bradford at 16.30 and arrived in Sheffield at 18.20 How long did the journey take?

	h	min
Arrived	18^{17}	20^{60}
Left	−16	30
	1	50

The journey took **1 hour 50 minutes**.

3 Find the time taken for each journey.

(a)	**Leave** Leeds	17.30	(b)	Sheffield	18.20	(c)	Leeds	19.30
	Arrive Nottingham	19.20		Coventry	20.55		Sheffield	20.20
(d)	**Leave** Sheffield	10.50	(e)	Leicester	12.15	(f)	Leeds	13.25
	Arrive Leicester	12.45		Rugby	13.05		Rugby	17.10

4 Find the time for each journey.

	(a)	(b)	(c)	(d)	(e)	(f)	(g)
Arrival time	12.15 pm	2 pm	9.30 pm	11.45 pm	7.10 pm	4 am	3.20 pm
Departure time	8.45 am	9.35 am	7.55 pm	7.50 am	3.25 pm	0.40 am	10.40 am

Ask your teacher if you should do Time Cards 61, 63, 65, 67, 69.

Tenths of a metre   0·1

Ten centimetres is one tenth of a metre.   10 cm = 0·1 m

Each tape shows 270 cm

2 m 70 cm = 2·7 m

7 0
2

2·7

1 Write each length in metres in decimal form.

(a) length of ruler
30 cm

(b) height of chair
1 m 20 cm

(c) width of table —130 cm—

(d) height of lamp post
5 m 40 cm

For questions 2 and 3 you need a metric tape or a metre stick marked in tenths of a metre.

2 This Textbook is about 0·3 m long. Check it by measuring.

3 **Work with a partner.**
Measure the lengths of these objects to the nearest **tenth of a metre**.
Record your answers in metres in decimal form.

(a) my waist   (b) my arm   (c) my height   (d) my chest
(e) width of teacher's desk   (f) width of my desk   (g) width of room

At a lamp post a trundle wheel counter shows   **134·7 m**
When pushed to the second lamp post it shows   **166·4 m**

Find the distance between lamp posts.

```
  166·4 m
– 134·7 m
   31·7 m
```
The distance is **31·7 m**

4 All the lamp posts are the same distance apart.
What will the counter show at:
(a) the third lamp post,   (b) the fourth lamp post,   (c) the fifth lamp post?

5 Find the difference between these trundle wheel distances:
(a) 248·5 m and 666·4 m,   (b) 89·7 m and 241·3 m,   (c) 354·6 m and 500·0 m

Six equally-spaced lamp posts span 162 m
What is the distance between posts?

```
    32·4 m
5)162·0 m
```
The distance is **32·4 m**

6 Eight equally-spaced lamp posts span 234·5 m. What is the distance between posts?

Hundredths of a metre

One centimetre is one hundredth of a metre.   1 cm = 0·01 m

| 35 cm = 0·35 m | 215 cm = 2·15 m | 1 m 4 cm = 1·04 m |

1 Write each length in metres in decimal form.

(a) 25 cm (b) 135 cm (c) 1 m 56 cm (d) 206 cm (e) 2 m 5 cm

You need a metre stick and a tape marked in centimetres.

2 Work with a partner.
Measure the lengths of these objects in centimetres.
Record your answers like this: **My waist is 52 cm or 0·52 m**
(a) my waist (b) my height (c) my arm (d) length of my desk
(e) width of teacher's desk (f) height of door (g) width of corridor

The washing machine is 0·65 m wide. The sink unit is 1·50 m wide.
Find the total width of the washing machine and the sink unit.

```
  0·65 m
+ 1·50 m
  2·15 m
```

Total width is **2·15 m**

wall
space

3 The kitchen is 4 m wide. What length of wall space, in metres, is left?

4 Would these pairs of units fit in this space? If they do fit, find what space is left.

(a)
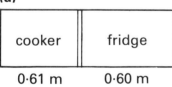

| cooker | fridge |
| 0·61 m | 0·60 m |

(b)

| cooker | freezer |
| 0·75 m | 1·25 m |

(c)
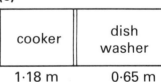

| cooker | dish washer |
| 1·18 m | 0·65 m |

Nine planks of wood, each 2·44 m long, are
used for the top of a fence.
What is the total length of the planks?

```
  2·44 m
  ×   9
 21·96 m
```

The total length is **21·96 m**

5 What is the total length of seven 1·83 m boards placed end to end?

6 A cupboard floor 1·05 m wide has 7 floor boards. What is the width of each board?

7 Find: (a) 67·44 m ÷ 6 (b) 8 × 6·49 m (c) 90·16 m ÷ 7 (d) 6 × 3·75 m

Distance charts

The numbers on the map show the distances between the towns in kilometres.

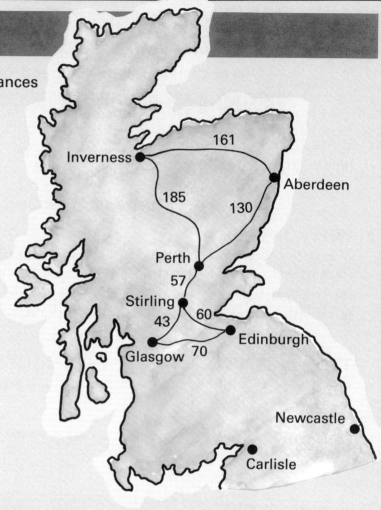

1 What is the **shortest** distance from
(a) Glasgow to Perth,
(b) Glasgow to Inverness,
(c) Edinburgh to Perth,
(d) Edinburgh to Aberdeen?

2 We can make a distance chart.
Copy and complete:

Distance between towns (km)

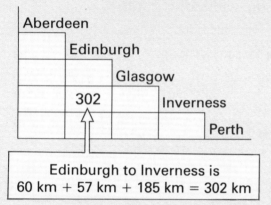

Edinburgh to Inverness is
60 km + 57 km + 185 km = 302 km

Here is another distance chart.
Use it to answer these questions.

3 Which two towns are
(a) 247 km apart,
(b) nearest each other,
(c) furthest apart?

4 How far is it from
(a) Aberdeen to Carmarthen,
(b) Dover to Glasgow,
(c) Fort William to Birmingham?

5 Which town is nearest to
(a) Birmingham,   (b) Dover,
(c) Fort William?

7 Copy this table and make a distance chart for your town and three other places.

Distance chart (km)

Aberdeen						
688	Birmingham					
835	212	Carmarthen				
952	325	473	Dover			
247	470	614	750	Edinburgh		
282	643	790	958	216	Fort William	
230	466	608	784	70	165	Glasgow

6 Which town is furthest from
(a) Birmingham,   (b) Carmarthen,
(c) Edinburgh?

Distance in kilometres

My town			
	Town A		
		Town B	
			Town C

Kilometres

> **Remember:** 1 kilometre = 1000 metres

1 Write these lengths in metres:
(a) $\frac{1}{2}$ km   (b) $\frac{1}{4}$ km   (c) $\frac{3}{4}$ km   (d) $1\frac{1}{4}$ km   (e) $1\frac{3}{4}$ km   (f) $2\frac{1}{2}$ km   (g) $2\frac{3}{4}$ km

2 Write these lengths in km like this: 1250 m = $1\frac{1}{4}$ km
(a) 1500 m (b) 2250 m (c) 750 m   (d) 500 m (e) 1750 m (f) 250 m   (g) 2500 m

> **100 m = one tenth of a kilometre** $\longrightarrow$ 100 m = 0·1 km

3 Write these lengths in km in decimal form:
(a) 400 m   (b) 900 m   (c) 1100 m (d) 700 m   (e) 1500 m (f) 2200 m (g) 4000 m

4 Write these lengths in metres:
(a) 0·1 km   (b) 0·3 km   (c) 0·5 km   (d) 0·8 km   (e) 1·2 km   (f) 2·5 km   (g) 2·7 km

5 This counter shows the distance travelled in kilometres by a car. $\longrightarrow$ `8 1 2 5·8`
(a) What will this counter show after a journey of 182·8 km?
(b) After a further journey the counter showed $\longrightarrow$ `8 5 0 3·2`
How far had the car travelled altogether on these two journeys?
(c) Is this distance more than from your school to Glasgow?

6 The distance from the Lighthouse to the Coastguard Station is 250 m or $\frac{1}{4}$ km.
Find the distance from
(a) the School to the Crossroads, (b) the Crossroads to Arden Cottages.

7 Which journey is longer and by how much? Answer in kilometres in decimal form.
(a) Crossroads to the Lighthouse **or** Post Office to the School.
(b) Arden Cottages to the Coastguard Station **or** Macbeth's Cave to the School.

8 (a) The teacher walks her dog from School to the Post Office, then on to the Castle, the Cave, and back along Hill Path. How long is this walk?
(b) Another walk is from School to the Crossroads, along the coast to Arden Cottages, and back by road to the School. How long is this walk?
(c) Which of these walks is longer and by how much?

Ask your teacher what to do next.

Finding areas

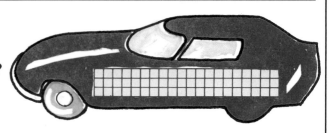

1 Look at the red grid on the car.
   (a) How many rows of squares are there?
   (b) How many squares are there in each row?
   (c) What is the area of the grid in squares?

2 (a) What is the area of this rectangle in square centimetres?
   (b) Copy the rectangle on centimetre squared paper and cut it out.
   (c) Cut along the diagonal to make two **right-angled triangles**.
   (d) Fit one triangle on top of the other. What is the area of each right-angled triangle?

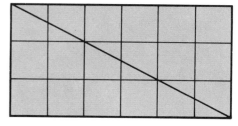

> The area of a right-angled triangle is **half** the area of its surrounding rectangle.

3 What is the area of each of these right-angled triangles?

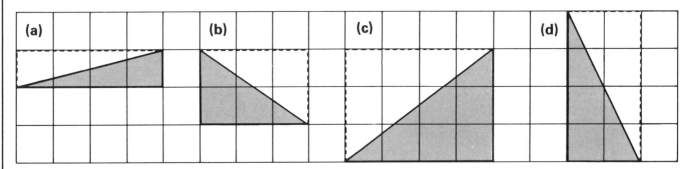

W **4** **Do Workbook Page 33**.

5 Copy and complete:

Area of rectangle **X** = _____ cm²
Area of right-angled triangle **Y** = _____ cm²
Area of the **whole** shape = _____ cm²

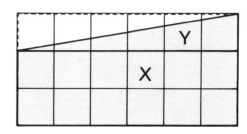

6 Find the area of each **whole** shape. Record in the same way as in question **5**.

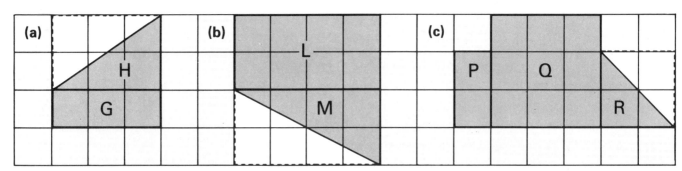

W **Do Workbook Pages 34, 35, and 36.**

Larger areas

You need four metre sticks.

1 **(a)** Make a square with the metre sticks.

(b) Could your desk top fit into this square?

(c) Could a car be parked in this square?

(d) What is the area of the square?

2 These sports surfaces have their lengths and breadths drawn to the nearest metre.

Each ☐ represents 1 square metre.

About what area is each of these sports surfaces?

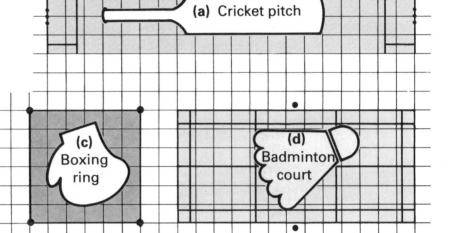

(a) Cricket pitch

(b) Squash court

(c) Boxing ring

(d) Badminton court

3 A car parking space is **about** 10 m² in area.
About how many cars could be parked on each of these surfaces?
(a) tennis court – 260 m² **(b)** football pitch – 7300 m² **(c)** rugby union pitch – 10 000 m²

An area of **10 000 m²** is called **1 hectare.**

4 The National Exhibition Centre in Birmingham covers 90 000 m².
What is this area in hectares?

5 The Scottish Exhibition Centre covers 2 hectares.
How many square metres is this area?

Ask your teacher what to do next.

Turning

Turning this way is **CLOCKWISE**

Turning this way is **ANTI-CLOCKWISE**

W

1 Cut out the clock and its hand from **Workbook Page 24**.
Stick them on a piece of cardboard.
Fix the hand to the clock with a paper fastener.

2 Set the hand of your clock at 12. Turn it clockwise to point to 3.
The hand has turned through 1 right angle clockwise.

3 Use the clock to help you.
Write the **number** the hand points to after each turn.

	Start at	Turn	Direction
(a)	12	2 right angles	clockwise
(b)	12	3 right angles	clockwise
(c)	12	4 right angles	clockwise
(d)	12	1 right angle	anti-clockwise
(e)	12	3 right angles	anti-clockwise

	Start at	Turn	Direction
(f)	6	1 right angle	clockwise
(g)	3	2 right angles	clockwise
(h)	9	3 right angles	anti-clockwise
(i)	6	4 right angles	anti-clockwise
(j)	3	3 right angles	clockwise

4 What is the **number of right angles** for a turn from
(a) 6 to 9 clockwise,   (b) 6 to 9 anti-clockwise,   (c) 3 to 9 anti-clockwise,
(d) 3 to 9 clockwise,   (e) 3 back to 3 clockwise,   (f) 9 to 12 anti-clockwise?

5 Write what the arrow will point to after each knob is turned.
(a) 3 right angles clockwise   (b) 2 right angles anti-clockwise   (c) 3 right angles anti-clockwise   (d) 1 right angle anti-clockwise

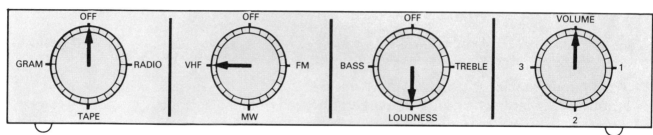

6 The swing door is seen from above in this drawing. ⟶
Make drawings to show the door after turning
from this position through
(a) 1 right angle anti-clockwise,
(b) 4 right angles clockwise,
(c) 3 right angles anti-clockwise.

Use tracing paper if you wish.

Degrees

Angles are often measured in units called **degrees**.
One degree is a very small turn.

This angle is **1 degree**.
We write this as **1°**.

1°

This amount of turning
is **10 degrees**.

10°

1 A right angle is 90 degrees. Copy and complete:

90°

Right angles	1	2	3	4
Degrees	90°			

2 The drawing shows a turning through 4 right angles. This angle has many names.
Draw an angle like this and copy the list of names beside your drawing.

a complete rotation   4 right angles
a revolution   360°
one full turn

3 Draw angles like these. Choose names from the list and write them
under the correct drawings.

$\frac{1}{4}$ turn   270°   2 right angles
$\frac{3}{4}$ turn   90°   3 right angles
$\frac{1}{2}$ turn   180°   1 right angle
                               a straight angle

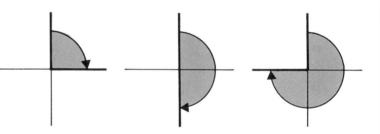

Use your cardboard clock to help you answer questions 4 and 5.

4 Write the number of **right angles** and the number of **degrees** for each rotation from
(a) 12 to 9 clockwise,   (b) 6 to 3 anti-clockwise,   (c) 3 to 9 clockwise,
(d) 6 to 12 clockwise,   (e) 12 to 9 anti-clockwise,   (f) 8 to 5 clockwise,
(g) 2 to 8 clockwise,   (h) 11 to 2 anti-clockwise,   (i) 4 to 10 anti-clockwise.

5 Write the number the hand points to after each turn:

	Start at	Turn
(a)	9	360° clockwise
(b)	3	90° clockwise
(c)	6	270° anti-clockwise

	Start at	Turn
(d)	1	180° anti-clockwise
(e)	5	90° clockwise
(f)	10	270° anti-clockwise

Compass directions

1 **(a)** **You need a gummed paper circle.** Fold it like this to make a compass.

Fold to make a right angle → Fold again to make a half right angle → Open out again

(b) Stick your compass on a page of your jotter. Draw lines along **two** of the folds for the directions North, South, East, and West. ──────→

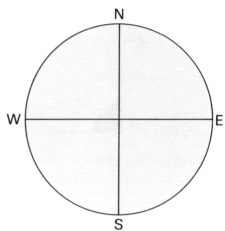

2 Rotate a pencil on top of your compass to help you do the questions below.
Write the direction you would be facing after each of these turns:

	Start facing	Rotation
(a)	N	1 right angle clockwise
(b)	N	3 right angles clockwise
(c)	E	2 right angles clockwise
(d)	S	3 right angles clockwise
(e)	S	90° clockwise
(f)	W	270° anti-clockwise
(g)	E	180° anti-clockwise
(h)	W	360° anti-clockwise

3 Draw lines along the other folds. Mark the directions North East, South East, South West, and North West.

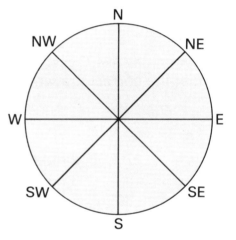

4 Make a list of the sizes of the angles below like this:

Angle	Right angles	Degrees	Rotation
A	1	90°	clockwise

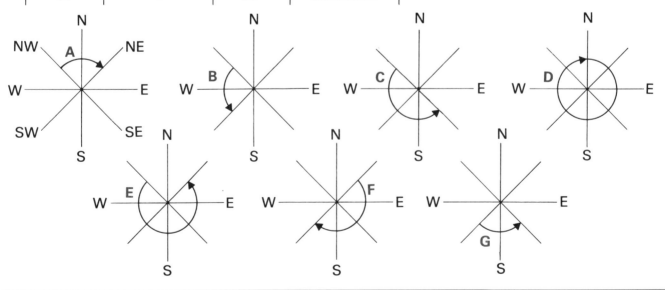

Cecil

Cecil is an odd centipede. He always crawls in a straight line. He uses only four directions – North, South, East, and West. When he turns he always makes right angles.

1 This is one of Cecil's crawls.

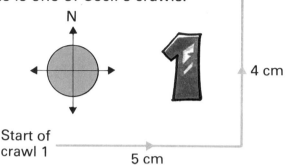

Finish

7 cm

4 cm

Start of crawl 1

5 cm

We can write the directions like this:

Crawl 1	5 cm East
	90° turn anti-clockwise
	4 cm North
	90° turn clockwise
	7 cm East

2 Write the directions for Crawl 2 and Crawl 3.

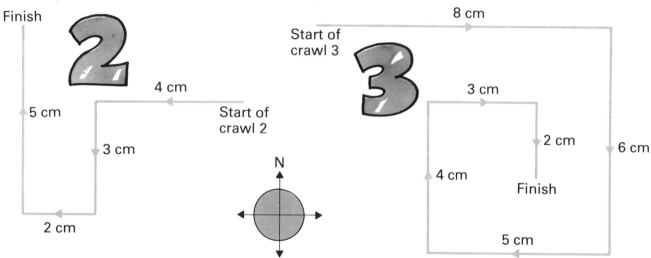

Finish

5 cm

4 cm

Start of crawl 2

3 cm

2 cm

N

Start of crawl 3

8 cm

3 cm

2 cm

6 cm

4 cm

Finish

5 cm

3 Cecil had a bad day when he did Crawl 4. He started and finished in the same place!

Use a ruler to measure in centimetres. Write instructions for Crawl 4.

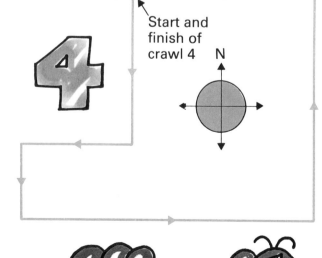

Start and finish of crawl 4

N

4 Some of the instructions for Crawl 5 are missing. Draw the crawl using a ruler and a right-angled corner. Write the complete instructions.

Crawl 5	3 cm North
	90° turn anti-clockwise
	8 cm ****
	90° turn ********
	5 cm South
	90° turn anti-clockwise
	4 cm ****
	90° turn ********
	7 cm North

Measuring angles in degrees

An **acute angle** is smaller than a right angle, less than 90°.

An **obtuse angle** is between 1 and 2 right angles, more than 90°, less than 180°.

This angle is larger than 180°. It is called a **reflex angle**. ⟶

W **1** Open your **Workbook at Page 24**. Is each angle acute, right, obtuse or reflex?

Record your answers like this: **Angle A   obtuse**

W **2** (a) Cut out the set of angles from **Workbook Page 24**.

(b) The large diagram below can be used to measure angles in degrees. Each interval is 10°.

> The corner of the angle must be at the centre of the diagram.
> One edge of the angle must lie along the 0° line.

Place angle **A** on top of the diagram as shown. Angle **A** is 110°.

(c) Measure the size of each angle. Record by adding to your answers for question 1:

Angle A   obtuse   110°
       B
       C

3 Write the size of each angle on the angle itself. Stick the angles in your jotter in increasing order of size.

A 110°

Spaceship Denon

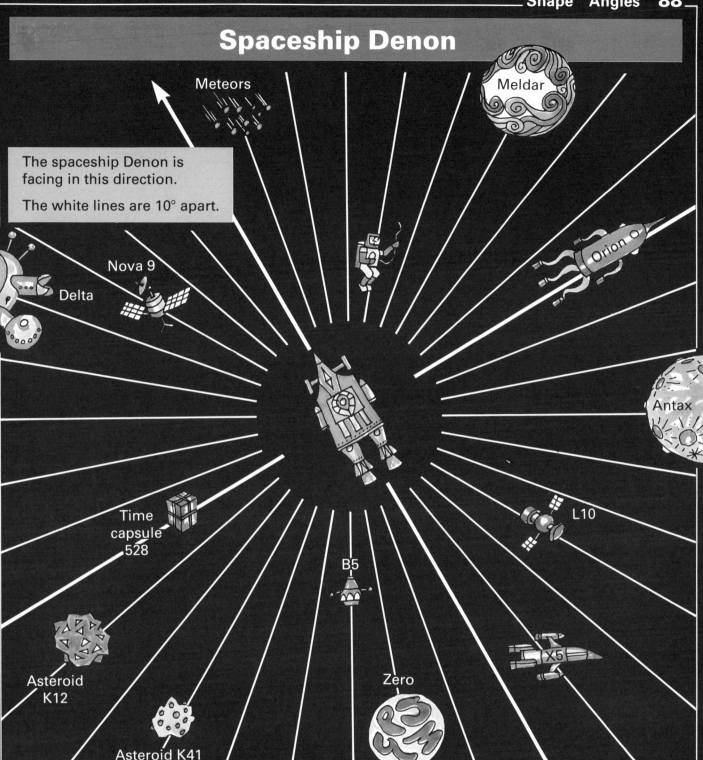

The spaceship Denon is facing in this direction.

The white lines are 10° apart.

Meteors

Meldar

Orion

Nova 9

Delta

Antax

Time capsule 528

L10

B5

Asteroid K12

X5

Zero

Asteroid K41

1 Turning anti-clockwise is turning to **PORT**. Turning clockwise is to **STARBOARD**.
Which object will Denon be pointing to if it turns, from this position,
- **(a)** 30° to Port,
- **(b)** 90° to Port,
- **(c)** 60° to Starboard,
- **(d)** 170° to Starboard,
- **(e)** 160° to Port,
- **(f)** 120° to Starboard?

2 What turn can Denon make to head in the direction of
- **(a)** Space Trader Orion,
- **(b)** Space Station Delta,
- **(c)** Lifeboat L10?

3 Write an order from Denon's Captain to the Helmsman to change course to
- **(a)** rescue the astronaut,
- **(b)** pass between asteroids K12 and K41,
- **(c)** service space beacon B5,
- **(d)** move directly away from the meteors.

Ask your teacher what to do next.

Part 4 Acknowledgements

p91. Rank Travel (x2), Intasun
      Canberra Cruises
p99. Thorn EMI Ferguson Ltd.
p101. RAF Museum
p103. National Bus Co.
p106. Barnaby Picture Library (x2), Allsport
p109. Oxprint

Part 4

Percentages

50% of the pens have been sold.
50% is read as 50 per cent.

50% means $\longrightarrow$ 50 out of 100

$\longrightarrow \frac{50}{100}$

$$50\% = \frac{50}{100}$$

1 Each large square has been divided into 100 equal parts.

For each large square, copy and complete:

$\frac{\blacksquare}{100}$ or $\blacksquare$ % is coloured.

$\frac{\blacksquare}{100}$ or $\blacksquare$ % is not coloured.

(a) **(b)** **(c)**

2 Each large triangle has been divided into 100 equal parts.

For each large triangle, find the percentage coloured red, , and blue.

(a) **(b)** **(c)**

100%

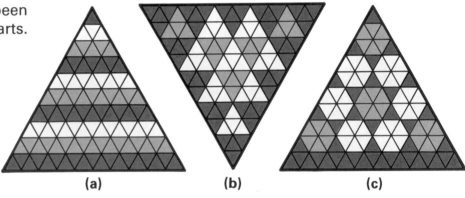

This rectangle has been divided into 100 equal squares.
100 out of the 100 squares have been coloured.
$\frac{100}{100}$ or 100% of the whole rectangle has been coloured.

100% of something means the whole of it.

3 Discuss these with your teacher:

(a)

100% PURE NEW WOOL

(b)
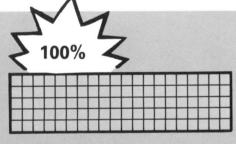
● 100% satisfaction or money refunded

(c)
100% WASHABLE – even in a machine

(d)
The centre forward was not 100% fit

Do Workbook Pages 38 and 39.

W

Using percentages

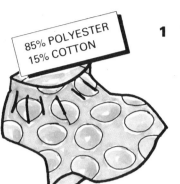

85% POLYESTER
15% COTTON

1 The material of this skirt is 85% polyester and 15% cotton.

Find the percentages missing from these labels:

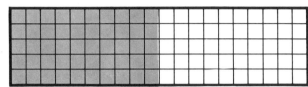

(a) | **80% wool**
■% nylon

(b) | ■% polyester
33% cotton

(c) | 50% POLYESTER
30% WOOL
■% COTTON

$\frac{50}{100}$ or 50% of this rectangle is red.

$$50\% = \frac{50}{100} = \frac{5}{10} = \frac{1}{2}$$

2 Do these in the same way:
   (a) 10%   **(b)** 20%   **(c)** 25%   **(d)** 75%   **(e)** 1%

Remember

$100\% = 1$ $50\% = \frac{1}{2}$ $25\% = \frac{1}{4}$ $75\% = \frac{3}{4}$
$20\% = \frac{1}{5}$ $10\% = \frac{1}{10}$ $1\% = \frac{1}{100}$

In a class of 28, 25% of the
children had chicken pox.
How many had chicken pox?

25% of $28 = \frac{1}{4}$ of $28 = 7$
7 children had chicken pox.

In the same way, find:

3 **(a)** 25% of 12   **(b)** 25% of 40   **(c)** 25% of 36   **(d)** 25% of 8

4 **(a)** 50% of 8   **(b)** 50% of 12   **(c)** 50% of 18   **(d)** 50% of 14

5 **(a)** 10% of 30   **(b)** 10% of 80   **(c)** 10% of 10   **(d)** 10% of 100

6 **(a)** 20% of 10   **(b)** 20% of 40   **(c)** 20% of 35   **(d)** 20% of 45

7 **(a)** How many girls are there in the class?
   (b) How many in the class take school lunch?
   (c) How many children do **not** wear glasses?
   (d) How many were absent last Tuesday?
   (e) How many were present?

About our class

There are **20** children in the class.

50% are girls.

25% take school lunch.

20% wear glasses.

10% were absent last Tuesday.

Do Workbook Page 40.

W

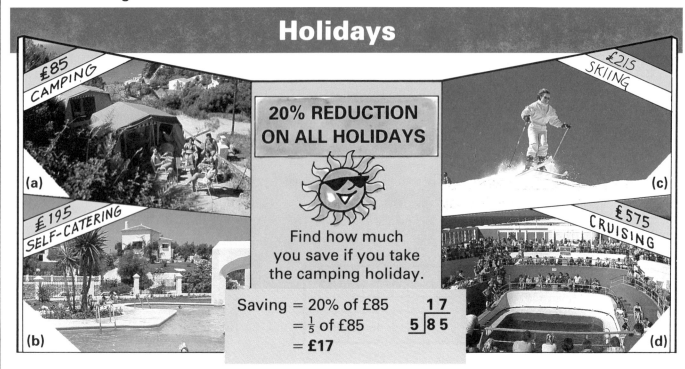

Holidays

£85 CAMPING (a)

£195 SELF-CATERING (b)

£215 SKIING (c)

£575 CRUISING (d)

20% REDUCTION ON ALL HOLIDAYS

Find how much you save if you take the camping holiday.

Saving = 20% of £85
= $\frac{1}{5}$ of £85
= **£17**

$$\begin{array}{r} 1\,7 \\ 5\overline{)8\,5} \end{array}$$

1 Now find the saving on each of the other holidays.

2 Susan had £80 and Errol had £96.
On holiday, Susan spent 25% of her money and Errol spent 50% of his.
How much did each spend?

3 Kay took £20 on holiday and spent £10% of this on postcards.
How much was this?

(a) £56

25% OFF ALL GOODS

(b) £48

(c) £64

(d)

(e) £100

(f) £132 £72

4 During a holiday, one of the shops reduced all prices by 25%.
Find the new price of each item. The first one is done for you.

Reduction on the watch = 25% of £56
= $\frac{1}{4}$ of £56
= £14

$$\begin{array}{r} 1\,4 \\ 4\overline{)5\,6} \end{array}$$

New price = £56 − £14
= **£42**

$$\begin{array}{r} 56 \\ -14 \\ \hline 42 \end{array}$$

5 On the last day of a holiday, the cost of the bus and boat trips were each reduced by 50%. Find the new fares for each trip.

BOAT TRIP £5

BUS TRIP £15

At the shops

The supermarket window shows the prices of items some time ago.
Since then, prices have gone up by 20%.
We can find the **increase in price** and the **new price** like this:

Increase in price = 20% of 95p
$= \frac{1}{5}$ of 95p
= **19p**

New price = 95p + 19p
= **£1·14**

```
  1 9
5 ⌐9 5
```

```
   95p
 + 19p
  114p
```

1 For each of the other items, find **(a)** the increase in price and **(b)** the new price.

2 Discuss these with your teacher:

3 These labels show the percentage increases
in weight or volume.
  (a) The choco used to weigh 50 g. Find its new weight.
  (b) The lemonade bottle used to contain 1 litre.
     Find its new volume.
  (c) The orange juice bottle used to contain 1 litre.
     Find its new volume.
  (d) Before the special offer, the sweets weighed 250 g.
     What is the new weight?
  (e) The ice-cream tub usually holds 500 ml.
     Find its new volume.

Ask your teacher what to do next.

Numbers in squares

967, 516, 349, 418, 352, 287.

This set of six 3-digit numbers can be arranged like this in a number square.

Across 349, 516, 287 **Down** 352, 418, 967.

3	4	9
5	1	6
2	8	7

1 Arrange each of these sets of six numbers to make a number square.
(a) 639, 562, 734, 578, 241, 891 (b) 816, 159, 672, 492, 834, 357
(c) 154, 514, 135, 341, 431, 315 (d) 644, 336, 764, 316, 714, 377

2 In a **magic square** the numbers along each row, column, and diagonal add to the same total. Which square in question **1** is magic?

5	4	9
10	6	2
3	8	7

3 This is another magic square.
(a) Find the total in any row, column or diagonal.
(b) What fraction of a row total is the number in the middle red square?
(c) Find the total of **all** the numbers.
(d) What fraction of this total is a row total?

4 Here are nine numbers which will make a magic square.

10   3   5   11   8   7   4   9   6

(a) Find the total of **all** the numbers.
(b) What will be the total in any row, column or diagonal?
(c) What will be the number in the middle square?
(d) Copy and complete the square.

5 (a) On squared paper, copy these numbered shapes and cut them out.
(b) Investigate how the shapes can be fitted together to make a magic square.

12
5
6
10
13
8 7
9
11

Number of squares

This shape is drawn on centimetre squared paper.

It has an $\boxed{\text{area}}$ of 4 cm² and a $\boxed{\text{perimeter}}$ of 10 cm.

1 For each shape below, find **(a)** its area, **(b)** its perimeter.
Make a table to record your answers like this ⟶

Shape	Area	Perimeter
A	8 cm²	14 cm
B		

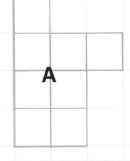
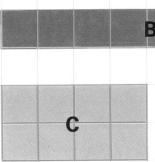
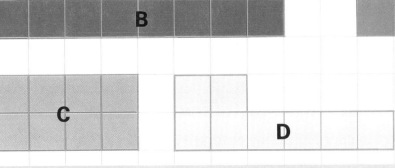

2 By drawing along the grid lines on centimetre squared paper, make as many different shapes as you can of area 6 cm².

3 Find the perimeter, in cm, of each of your shapes.
What is **(a)** your longest perimeter, **(b)** your shortest perimeter?

4 For each shape below, find **(a)** its perimeter, **(b)** its area.
Make a table to record your answers like this ⟶

Shape	Perimeter	Area
P	14 cm	8 cm²

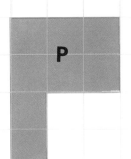
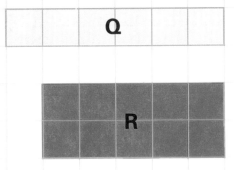
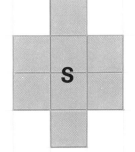
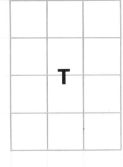

5 By drawing along the grid lines on centimetre squared paper, make as many different shapes as you can of perimeter 12 cm.

6 Find the area, in cm², of each of your shapes.
What is **(a)** your largest area, **(b)** your smallest area?

Ask your teacher if you should do Investigation Cards 52, 54, 56, 58, 60.

Sharing

45 sweets have to be shared equally among 13 children. How many does each child get?

This means that 45 has to be divided by 13.

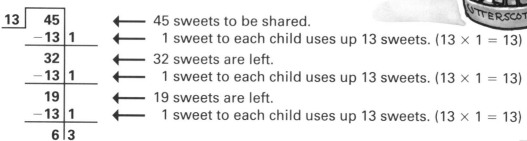

```
13 │  45        ◄──── 45 sweets to be shared.
    │ −13 │1    ◄────  1 sweet to each child uses up 13 sweets. (13 × 1 = 13)
    │  32        ◄──── 32 sweets are left.
    │ −13 │1    ◄────  1 sweet to each child uses up 13 sweets. (13 × 1 = 13)
    │  19        ◄──── 19 sweets are left.
    │ −13 │1    ◄────  1 sweet to each child uses up 13 sweets. (13 × 1 = 13)
    │   6 │3
```

Each child gets **3** sweets and there are 6 sweets left over.   45 ÷ 13 = 3 r 6

1 In the same way, find how many sweets each child gets and what is left over.

	(a)	(b)	(c)	(d)
Number of sweets	44	39	73	80
Number of children	17	13	20	24

2 Thirty sweets are shared equally among 13 girls.
How many sweets does each get and how many are left over?

3 Find: **(a)** 19⟌38 **(b)** 26⟌53 **(c)** 31⟌85 **(d)** 37⟌111 **(e)** 40⟌130

---

15 people have to share £180 equally. How much does each person receive?

This means that 180 has to be divided by 15.

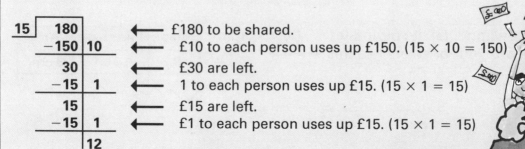

```
15 │  180         ◄──── £180 to be shared.
    │ −150 │10    ◄──── £10 to each person uses up £150. (15 × 10 = 150)
    │   30         ◄──── £30 are left.
    │  −15 │ 1    ◄──── 1 to each person uses up £15. (15 × 1 = 15)
    │   15         ◄──── £15 are left.
    │  −15 │ 1    ◄──── £1 to each person uses up £15. (15 × 1 = 15)
    │       │12
```

Each person receives **£12**.   180 ÷ 15 = 12

4 In the same way find how much each person receives.

	(a)	(b)	(c)	(d)
Number of £	176	228	300	468
Number of people	16	19	25	36

5 £168 is shared equally among 14 people.
How much does each person get?

6 Two hundred and forty £1 coins are shared equally among 21 people.
How much does each receive and how many £1 coins are left over?

7 Find: **(a)** 121 ÷ 11 **(b)** 276 ÷ 23 **(c)** 412 ÷ 34 **(d)** 600 ÷ 45 **(e)** 728 ÷ 56

More sharing

**380 curtain hooks are shared equally among 18 curtains.
How many hooks does each curtain have and how many are left over?**

```
18 | 380
     -180 | 10      ← 380 hooks to be shared.
     ─────           ← 10 hooks to each curtain uses up 180 hooks. (18 × 10 = 180)
      200            ← 200 hooks are left.
     -180 | 10      ← 10 hooks to each curtain uses up 180 hooks. (18 × 10 = 180)
     ─────
       20            ← 20 hooks are left.
      -18 | 1        ← 1 hook to each curtain uses up 18 hooks. (18 × 1 = 18)
     ─────
        2 |21
```

Each curtain has **21** hooks and there are 2 hooks left over.   380 ÷ 18 = 21 r 2

1 In the same way find how many hooks each curtain has and what is left over.

	(a)	(b)	(c)	(d)
Number of hooks	218	462	576	740
Number of curtains	18	22	26	32

2 Fifteen people have to share £315 equally. How much does each person get?

3 A girl has to save £2·64 in 12 weeks. How many **pence** should she save per week?

4 How many days are there in 768 hours?

5 How many hours are there in 1320 minutes?

6 Find: **(a)** 14 ⟌182   **(b)** 19 ⟌385   **(c)** 23 ⟌483   **(d)** 25 ⟌777   **(e)** 33 ⟌1089

**In a competition, the total amount to be shared among the winners is £2553.
There were 23 people who gave the correct answer.
How much does each receive?**

```
23 | 2553
    -2300 | 100      ← £2553 to be shared.
    ──────            ← £100 to each person uses up £2300. (23 × 100 = 2300)
      253             ← £253 are left.
     -230 | 10        ← £10 to each person uses up £230. (23 × 10 = 230)
    ──────
       23             ← £23 are left.
      -23 | 1         ← £1 to each person uses up £23. (23 × 1 = 23)
    ──────
          |111
```

Each person receives **£111**.   2553 ÷ 23 = 111

7 Prize money of £1568 is shared equally among 14 winners. How much does each receive?

8 Four thousand cucumber seeds are shared equally among 36 packets. How many seeds are in each packet and how many are left over?

9 Are the answers to these **more** or **less** than 100?
(a) 1820 ÷ 18   **(b)** 4301 ÷ 42   **(c)** 5513 ÷ 59   **(d)** 3825 ÷ 36   **(e)** 6030 ÷ 61

10 Find: **(a)** 2210 ÷ 22   **(b)** 3350 ÷ 33   **(c)** 7659 ÷ 69   **(d)** 6415 ÷ 53

Do Workbook Page 41.   W

Forming teams

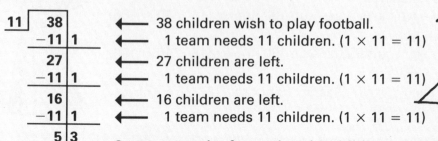

This means that 38 has to be divided by 11.

```
 11 | 38
    -11 | 1      ⟵  38 children wish to play football.
                 ⟵   1 team needs 11 children. (1 × 11 = 11)
      27          ⟵  27 children are left.
    -11 | 1      ⟵   1 team needs 11 children. (1 × 11 = 11)
      16          ⟵  16 children are left.
    -11 | 1      ⟵   1 team needs 11 children. (1 × 11 = 11)
       5 | 3
```

3 teams can be formed and 5 children are left over.   38 ÷ 11 = 3 r 5

1 How many football teams of 11 can be formed and how many children are left over if there are **(a)** 29 children,

   (b) 42 children?

2 There are 24 players in a bowling team. How many teams can be formed from 75 players?

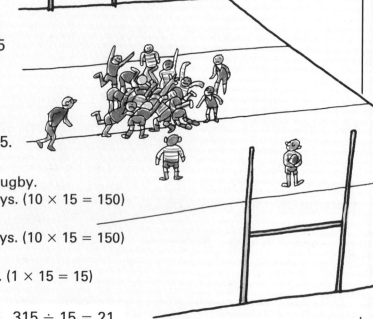

This means that 315 has to be divided by 15.

```
 15 | 315
   -150 | 10     ⟵  315 boys wish to play rugby.
                 ⟵    10 teams need 150 boys. (10 × 15 = 150)
     165          ⟵  165 boys are left.
   -150 | 10     ⟵    10 teams need 150 boys. (10 × 15 = 150)
      15          ⟵  15 boys are left.
    -15 | 1      ⟵    1 team needs 15 boys. (1 × 15 = 15)
        | 21
```

21 teams can be formed.   315 ÷ 15 = 21

3 At another school 195 boys wish to play rugby. How many teams of 15 can be formed?

4 Two hundred and forty-five girls put their names down for hockey. How many teams of 11 can be formed and how many girls are left over?

5 A box can hold 24 pencils. How many boxes can be filled from 768 pencils?

6 A bar of chocolate costs 24p. How many bars can be bought for £5 and how much money is left?

7 A car uses 1 litre of petrol to travel 14 kilometres. How many litres will be needed for a journey of 1554 kilometres?

8 A space satellite has been in orbit for 5620 hours. How many **complete** days is this?

Division with a calculator

A job was advertised as paying a yearly salary of **£9256**.
How much is this per week?

This means that 9256 has to be divided by 52.

Enter 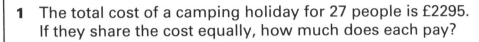 178.

The salary is **£178** per week.

1 The total cost of a camping holiday for 27 people is £2295.
If they share the cost equally, how much does each pay?

2 A doctor's prescription requires that 15 pills are taken every day.
How many days will 465 pills last?

3 Find: **(a)** 1026 ÷ 18   **(b)** 1771 ÷ 23   **(c)** 1849 ÷ 43   **(d)** 2430 ÷ 45   **(e)** 6534 ÷ 66

4 Cabbage plants are tied in bundles of 25.
Leek plants are tied in bundles of 75.
A gardener needs 300 cabbage plants
and 600 leeks.
How many **(a)** bundles of cabbages,
(b) bundles of leeks does he buy?

5 Jim has a packet of weedkiller for his grass. The directions say
it has to be applied at 30 g per square metre. If the weedkiller
weighs 750 g, how many square metres can he treat?

6 A large store has 26 departments. There is a
Christmas tree in each department.
The store has the following decorations:

Silver Tinsel	– 390 m	Gold Tinsel	– 650 m
Silver Bells	– 312	Red Bells	– 286
Chocolate Santas	– 494	Blue Stars	– 572

These decorations are shared equally among the 26 trees.
Make a list of the decorations on each tree.

Record like this: Silver Tinsel – ■ m

7 Which is greater: **(a)** 672 ÷ 21 *or* 986 ÷ 34,   **(b)** 648 ÷ 18 *or* 784 ÷ 28?

8 **(a)** Divide 729 by 27. Is 729 a **square number**?
(b) Divide 1224 by 34. Is 1224 a **square number**?

9 Tim has 800 bricks and 1½ tonnes of sand delivered to his front gate.
(a) His barrow holds 25 bricks.
How many journeys are needed to move the bricks to his back garden?
(b) His barrow holds 75 kg of sand. How many journeys are needed?

Money and the calculator

The cost of renting a T.V. set is £135 for 1 year.
How much is this per month?

This means that we have to divide 135 by 12.

Enter [1] [3] [5] [÷] [1] [2] [=] ⟶ **11.25**

The cost is **£11·25** per month.

1 The following is the cost of renting each of
three video recorders for 1 year: mono recorder – £189
stereo recorder – £210
hi-fi recorder   – £243

(a) Calculate the cost of renting each recorder for 1 month.

(b) Find the difference in price in monthly rental between
the dearest and the cheapest recorder.

A group train ticket for 14 children costs £8·68.
How much did they each pay?

Enter [8] [·] [6] [8] [÷] [1] [4] [=] ⟶ **0.62**

Each child pays **62p**.

2 Sixteen packets of Snappies cost £2·72. What is the price of 1 packet?

3 Twelve packets of Soapo cost £56·64. What is the price of 1 packet?

4 For Remembrance Day, 28 children collected money in the Town Centre.
The boys collected £82·40 and the girls collected £93·44.
What was the average sum collected per child?

5 Mr W. Arm uses only gas and electricity in his home. His
annual gas bill is £761·28 and his annual electricity bill is
£302·64. What does he pay on average each **week** for
(a) gas,   (b) electricity,   (c) fuel?

To find 476 ÷ 41:

Enter [4] [7] [6] [÷] [4] [1] [=] ⟶ **11.609756**

This answer can be shown on a number line.

The answer to 476 ÷ 41 is between 11 and 12.   11 ———————————— 12

6 Which of these have answers between 11 and 12?

(a) 476 ÷ 42   (b) 476 ÷ 39   (c) 476 ÷ 40   (d) 476 ÷ 43   (e) 476 ÷ 44

Do Workbook Page 42.

Thinking about answers

Here are three questions:

Q

1 **170** sweets are shared among **11** boys. How many sweets does each boy get?

2 How many teams of **11** can be formed from **170** boys?

3 How many minibuses, each holding **11** boys, are needed to transport **170** boys?

The answer to each question can be found by dividing 170 by 11.

Use a calculator to check that 170 ÷ 11 = `15.454545`

We have to think about the problem to decide whether each answer is 15 or 16.

A

1 Each boy gets **15** sweets.

2 **15** teams can be formed.

3 **16** minibuses are needed.

1 A **lunar** month has 28 days. How many **complete** lunar months are there in 365 days?

2 How many **complete** pages of 24 stamps can be filled from a total of 700 stamps?

3 A cinema sweet store has:

    260 cartons of lemon juice   400 chocolate ices
    300 cartons of orange juice   325 tubs of ice cream

These are shared equally among 18 usherettes.
Make a list of what each usherette has on her tray.

4 A bus can hold 31 children. How many of these buses are needed to take 136 children on a bus trip?

5 A walker has a pace of 85 cm. How many paces are required to walk a distance of 50 metres?

6 A classroom has a length of 14 m 13 cm. Square tiles of edge length 30 cm are laid along this length. How many tiles are needed?

7

Wool for knitting is sold in **hanks**.

38 hanks are needed to knit an anorak.
13 hanks are needed to knit a jacket.
42 hanks are needed to knit a cardigan.

How many **(a)** anoraks,   **(b)** jackets,   **(c)** cardigans, can be knitted from 1000 hanks?

8

42 dresses can be knitted from 1000 hanks.
15 pullovers can be knitted from 500 hanks.
136 jerkins can be knitted from 2000 hanks.

How many hanks are needed to knit **(a)** a dress,   **(b)** a pullover,   **(c)** a jerkin?

Famine relief

Use a calculator.

To collect money for famine relief, Mr B. Lister walked from John O'Groats to Land's End. The total distance was 1406 kilometres (874 miles).
It took 25 days to walk this total distance and he collected £380 000.

1 Find:

(a) to the nearest kilometre, the average distance walked each day,

(b) to the nearest mile, the average distance walked each day,

(c) the average amount of money collected each day.

2 A class of 29 pupils decide to collect money for famine relief from a Raffle and a Jumble Sale.

The children

sell	**2700**	Raffle Tickets,
distribute	**2500**	Jumble Sale leaflets,
collect	**£840**.	

On average

(a) about how many raffle tickets does each child sell,

(b) about how many leaflets does each child distribute,

(c) how much does each child collect, to the nearest £?

3 An aircraft can carry a total weight of 23 tonnes. The following have to be transported to a famine area:

Food — 203 tonnes   Medicine — 30 tonnes
Clothing — 12 tonnes   Toys — 8 tonnes

How many aircraft are required?

4 An African famine centre had the following goods to distribute to 15 villages:

1425 bags of flour	720 tents
30 000 blankets	480 kg of medical supplies
36 000 tins of dried milk	6 tonnes of rice

If these goods are shared equally among 15 trucks, list the goods carried by each truck.

Record like this: tents — ■

Ask your teacher if you should do Number Cards 31, 33, 35, 37, 39.

Scale drawings

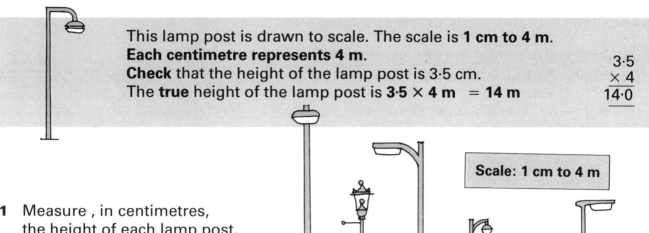

This lamp post is drawn to scale. The scale is **1 cm to 4 m**.
Each centimetre represents 4 m.
Check that the height of the lamp post is 3·5 cm.
The **true** height of the lamp post is **3·5 × 4 m = 14 m**

$$\begin{array}{r} 3\cdot 5 \\ \times\ 4 \\ \hline 14\cdot 0 \\ \hline \end{array}$$

1 Measure , in centimetres,
the height of each lamp post.

2 Calculate the true height of
each lamp post.

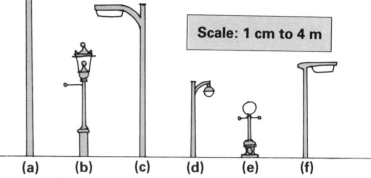

Scale: 1 cm to 4 m

(a)   (b)   (c)   (d)   (e)   (f)

3 The scale used for the street below is **1 cm to 5 m**.
- **(a)** Measure the drawing in centimetres and then
calculate the true height of each building.
- **(b)** How much higher are the Skye Flats than the Hotel Ritz?
- **(c)** How far apart, in **metres**, are the lamp posts?
- **(d)** What is the true width of the frontage of Sparks Stores?
- **(e)** What is the true width of the Palace?

Scale: 1 cm to 5 m

4 **(a)** Measure the drawings below and then calculate the true height of each building.
(b) List the buildings in order of height.

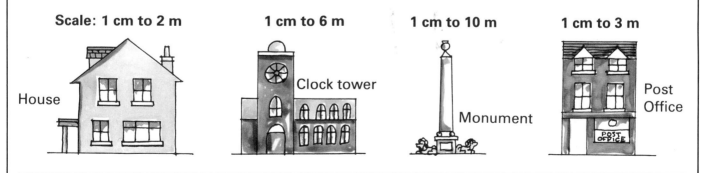

Scale: 1 cm to 2 m   1 cm to 6 m   1 cm to 10 m   1 cm to 3 m

House   Clock tower   Monument   Post Office

Scale models

This aeroplane is drawn using a scale of **1 cm to 5 m**.

1 **(a)** What is the true length of the aeroplane?
   (b) What is its true wingspan?

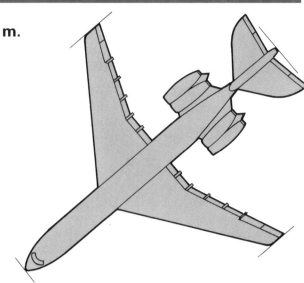

The tanker scale is **1 cm to 30 m**.

2 What is the true length of the tanker?

3 **(a)** Which is longer, the real aeroplane
        or the real tanker?
   (b) How many times as long?

4 A bus is 9 metres long.
   How many buses match the length of
   (a) the aeroplane,   **(b)** the tanker?

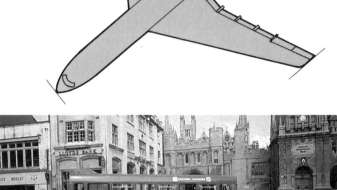

These cars are drawn using a scale of **1 cm to 50 cm**.

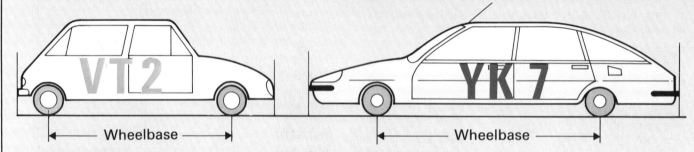

Wheelbase   Wheelbase

5 Measure the lengths of these drawings in centimetres.
   Calculate the true length of each car in   **(a)** centimetres,   **(b)** metres.

6 How much longer is the YK7 than the VT2?

7 Find the true wheelbase for each car in   **(a)** centimetres,   **(b)** metres.

8 How high is the top of the YK7s aerial above the ground?

9 How many YK7s placed bumper to bumper would match the length of the aeroplane?

10 Are fifty VT2s longer than the tanker? Find the difference in length.

11 **(a)** What is the length of your playground?
    (b) Would the length of the real aeroplane fit into the length of your playground?
    (c) Would the length of the real tanker fit?
    (d) How many YK7s would fit the length of your playground?

Flight distances

THETA

BETA

DELTA

GAMMA

Ulna

OMEGA

ALPHA

Scale: 1 cm to 75 km

You may use a calculator for this page.

1 Each red dot shows the position of an oilrig.
Find the true distance of each oilrig from the shorebase Ulna.
Which two rigs are the same distance from Ulna?

2 Name the rig which is furthest from rig ALPHA.
How far is it from ALPHA?

3 If a helicopter based on BETA flies to OMEGA, then on to ALPHA,
and then back to BETA, how far does it fly?

4 About how far is it from THETA to
   (a) DELTA,   **(b)** ALPHA?

The lines on this map show
flight paths from Glasgow to
places in Europe.

5 Find the distances from Glasgow
by air to the five other places
on the map.

6 The distance by road from
Glasgow to Vienna is 2050 km.
How much further is this than
the flight distance?

7 About how far is it from
Gibraltar to Rome by air?

8 About how far does a pilot
and his crew fly when
they travel from Glasgow
to Rome, Rome to Gibraltar,
and then back to Glasgow?

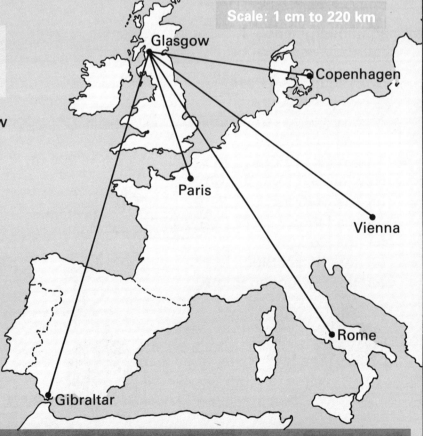

Scale: 1 cm to 220 km

Glasgow

Copenhagen

Paris

Vienna

Rome

Gibraltar

Rivers and roads

You need a ruler and a length of pipecleaner or string or thread.

The road and the river are drawn to a scale of **1 cm to 40 km**.

1 Which is longer, the red road or the blue river? How much longer?

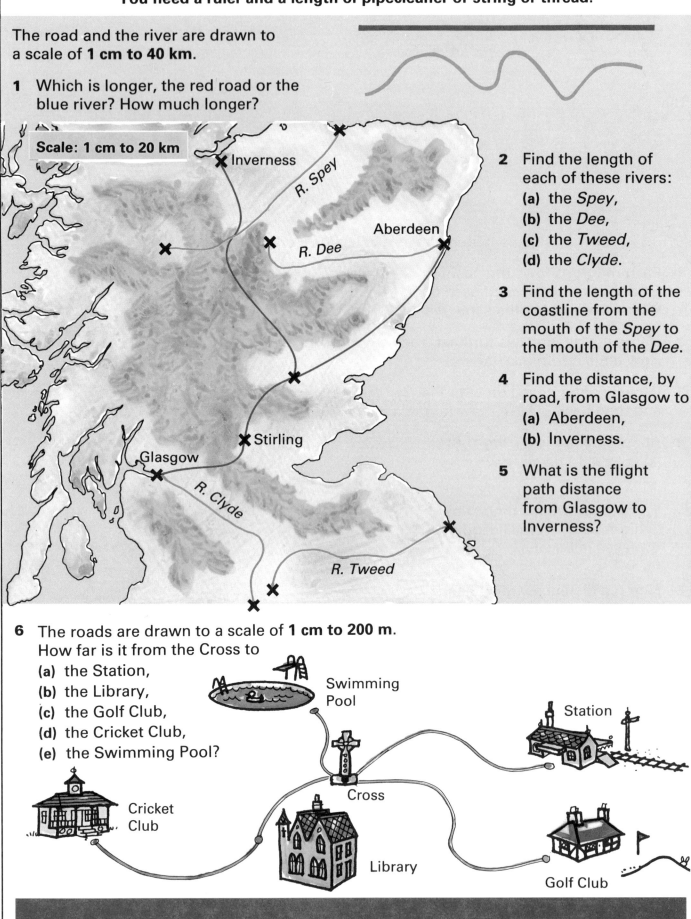

Scale: 1 cm to 20 km

2 Find the length of each of these rivers:
(a) the *Spey*,
(b) the *Dee*,
(c) the *Tweed*,
(d) the *Clyde*.

3 Find the length of the coastline from the mouth of the *Spey* to the mouth of the *Dee*.

4 Find the distance, by road, from Glasgow to
(a) Aberdeen,
(b) Inverness.

5 What is the flight path distance from Glasgow to Inverness?

6 The roads are drawn to a scale of **1 cm to 200 m**. How far is it from the Cross to
(a) the Station,
(b) the Library,
(c) the Golf Club,
(d) the Cricket Club,
(e) the Swimming Pool?

Drawing to scale

Here are the **true** heights of some trees:

Ash 28 m   Monkey Puzzle 26 m
Elm 36 m   Willow 22 m
Oak 24 m   Poplar 42 m
                              Pear 18 m

To draw the height of the Pear tree to a scale
of **1 cm to 4 m**, we calculate the scaled height of the tree.

   4 m is represented by 1 cm
   18 m is represented by 18 ÷ 4
                              = 4·5 cm

The scaled height of the tree is **4·5 cm**.

We draw a line to represent the height of the tree
The rest of the tree is not drawn to scale.

1   Make scale drawings of the other trees
using a scale of **1 cm to 4m**.

2   Make scale drawings of these shot puts
using a scale of **1 cm to 2 m**:

Farina 20 m   Natalia 22 m   Ingmar 19 m
Carmel 17 m   Tania 16 m   Helina 21 m

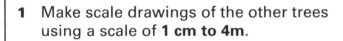

Record your answers like this:
   Tania _____

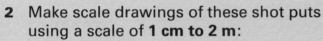

3 Work as a group.

Here are the heights of some mountains in metres.

Scafell Pike   950 m   Zugspitze   3000 m
Snowdon   1050 m   Matterhorn 4500 m
Ben Nevis   1350 m   Mont Blanc 4800 m

Use a scale of **1 cm to 100 m**.
Make drawings of these
mountains with the **heights**
drawn to scale. Sketch the
rest of each mountain.
Colour, label, and cut out
your mountains to make a
wall display.

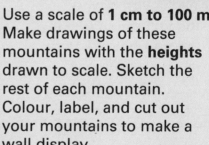

Do Workbook Pages 43 and 44.

W

Layers

You need centimetre cubes.

1 Build each of these shapes using your cubes. Write the volume of each in cm³.

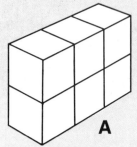
A

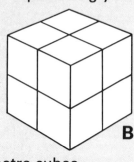
B

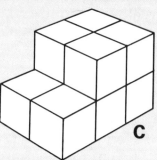
C

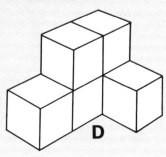
D

2 You need 24 centimetre cubes.
Use **all** of the cubes to build a cuboid **P** with a **bottom layer** like this:

Copy this table and complete the first part for cuboid **P**.

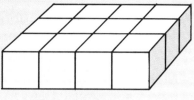
bottom layer of **P**

Cuboid	Volume of one layer (cm³)	Number of layers	Volume of cuboid (cm³)
P			24
Q			
R			
S			

3 Repeat question **2** for cuboids **Q**, **R**, and **S** with **bottom layers** like these:

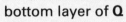
bottom layer of **Q**

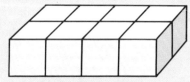
bottom layer of **R**

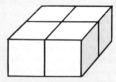
bottom layer of **S**

We can find the volume of a cuboid like this:
Multiply the volume of one layer by the number of layers.

4 Cuboids **T**, **V**, and **W** are built with centimetre cubes.
For each cuboid write:
(a) the volume of one layer,
(b) the number of layers,
(c) its total volume.

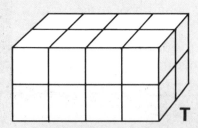
T

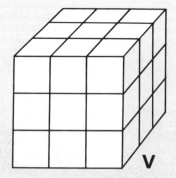
V

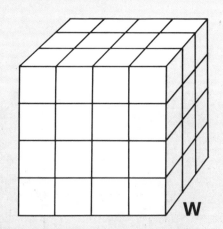
W

Filling boxes

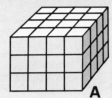

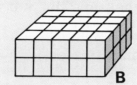

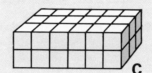

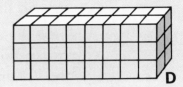

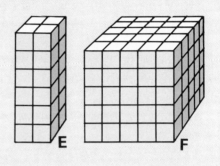

1 These cuboids are built with **centimetre cubes**.
Copy and complete a table like this.

Cuboid	A	B	C	D	E	F
Volume of one layer (cm³)						
Number of layers						
Volume of cuboid (cm³)						

2 The bottom of this box is covered with
one layer of centimetre cubes.
- **(a)** What is the volume of this layer of
cubes?
- **(b)** Another layer is needed to
completely fill the box.
What is the volume of the box?

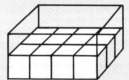

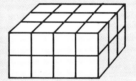

3

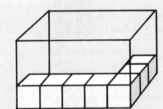

Centimetre cubes are placed inside this box.
Five cubes fit along its length and 3 cubes along its breadth.
- **(a)** What would be the volume of one complete layer of
cubes covering the bottom of the box?
- **(b)** Three layers of cubes are required to completely fill the box.
What is the volume of the box in cm³?

4 Centimetre cubes have been placed along the inside edges of this box.
- **(a)** How many cubes fit along its length?
- **(b)** How many cubes fit along its breadth?
- **(c)** What would be the volume of one complete layer of
cubes covering the bottom of the box?
- **(d)** How many layers would be required to completely fill
the box?
- **(e)** What is the volume of the box in cm³?

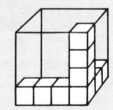

5 This box has a **square** bottom with edges 8 cm long.
Centimetre cubes are fitted along an inside edge as shown.
- **(a)** How many cubes fit along this edge?
- **(b)** What would be the volume of the bottom layer of cubes?
- **(c)** Altogether six layers are required to fill the box.
What is the volume of the box?
- **(d)** What volume of sand would completely fill three boxes?

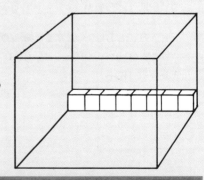

Volume of containers

You need the plastic box, centimetre cubes, and the measuring jug.

1 (a) Lay centimetre cubes along the inside edges of the box like this.
   (b) How many would you need to cover the bottom completely?
   (c) What is the volume of this bottom layer?
   (d) How many layers would be required to completely fill the box?
   (e) What is the volume of the box in cm³?

2 (a) Empty the cubes out of the box.
   (b) Pour 1 litre of water into the box.
   (c) Does it take more than 1 litre **or** less than 1 litre, **or** about 1 litre of water to completely fill the box?

> 1000 cm³ is the same volume as 1 litre (1000 ml)
> 1 cm³ is the same volume as 1 ml

3 Write these volumes in the other way:
   (a) 25 cm³   (b) 250 ml   (c) 150 ml   (d) 60 cm³   (e) 700 ml   (f) 910 cm³

4 Write the volume of each of these containers in the other way.

560 ml   50 ml   300 ml   120 cm³   750 cm³   180 cm³   75 ml   500 ml   100 cm³

5 Write each of these volumes in cm³:
   (a) 1500 ml   (b) 4 litres   (c) 5·5 litres   (d) 9 litres 250 ml   (e) 10 litres 50 ml

6 A sand bucket has a volume of 10 000 cm³. How many litres of water can it hold?

7 A water bucket has a volume of 8 litres. How many cubic centimetres of sand can it hold?

Ask your teacher what to do next.

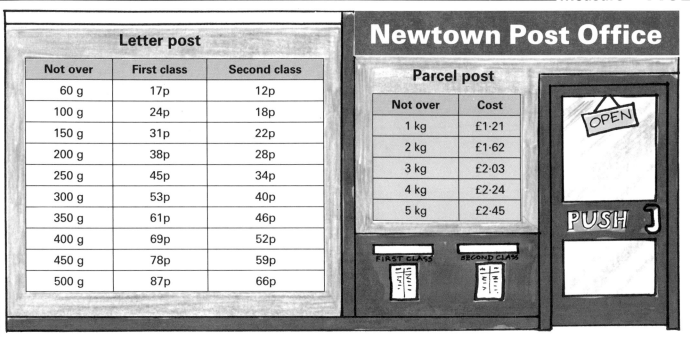

Letter post

Not over	First class	Second class
60 g	17p	12p
100 g	24p	18p
150 g	31p	22p
200 g	38p	28p
250 g	45p	34p
300 g	53p	40p
350 g	61p	46p
400 g	69p	52p
450 g	78p	59p
500 g	87p	66p

Newtown Post Office

Parcel post

Not over	Cost
1 kg	£1·21
2 kg	£1·62
3 kg	£2·03
4 kg	£2·24
5 kg	£2·45

FIRST CLASS   SECOND CLASS

1 **Use the tables** to find what it costs to post the following:

Letters (1st class) weighing   **(a)** 150 g,   **(b)** 270 g,   **(c)** 440 g,   **(d)** 45 g,
Letters (2nd class) weighing   **(e)** 100 g,   **(f)** 310 g,   **(g)** 490 g,   **(h)** 35 g,
Parcels weighing   **(i)** 3 kg,   **(j)** 1 kg 350 g,   **(k)** 4 kg 150 g,   **(l)** 3 kg 500 g.

The Flitt family moved to a new house.
They went to the post office to post letters and parcels.

2 Dad returned books by parcel post to the library.
The parcel weighed 2 kg 450 g. How much did it cost to post?

3 Mum sent a $1\frac{1}{2}$ kg box of biscuits to Grandma. What did it cost to post?

4 Jill returned some cassettes, total weight 210 g, to a friend.
What did it cost by second class letter post?

5 The Flitts sent 50 letters to tell friends their new address.
None of the letters weighed more than 60 g.
What was the total cost of the second class stamps?

6 John has two friends who are twins. He sends each
a book, weighing 460 g, as a birthday present.
   (a) Is it cheaper to send the books **separately by
   second class post** or as **one parcel**?
   (b) What is the difference in postage?

7 Susan wishes to send a gift to six friends by letter post.
Each gift weighs 85 g. How much change will she get from £5 if
she sends them **(a)** first class,   **(b)** second class?

8 **You need the parcels A, B, C, and D and scales.**
Copy and complete the table.

Parcel	A	B	C	D
Weight				
Cost of stamps				

Rail fares

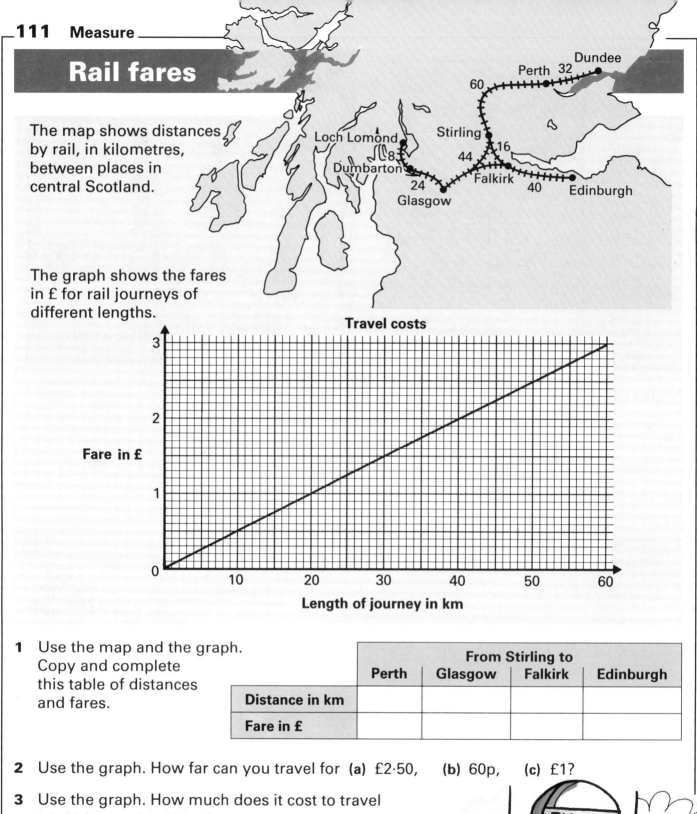

The map shows distances by rail, in kilometres, between places in central Scotland.

The graph shows the fares in £ for rail journeys of different lengths.

1 Use the map and the graph. Copy and complete this table of distances and fares.

	From Stirling to			
	Perth	**Glasgow**	**Falkirk**	**Edinburgh**
Distance in km				
Fare in £				

2 Use the graph. How far can you travel for **(a)** £2·50, **(b)** 60p, **(c)** £1?

3 Use the graph. How much does it cost to travel
(a) 30 km, (b) 10 km?

4 **Calculate** how much it costs to travel 1 km.
Use this cost to help you to answer questions **5** and **6**.

5 Find the fares from Glasgow to
(a) Dumbarton, (b) Loch Lomond, (c) Dundee.

6 Look at the notice board showing fares from Edinburgh.
Calculate the length of the journey from Edinburgh to
(a) Glasgow, (b) Dundee.

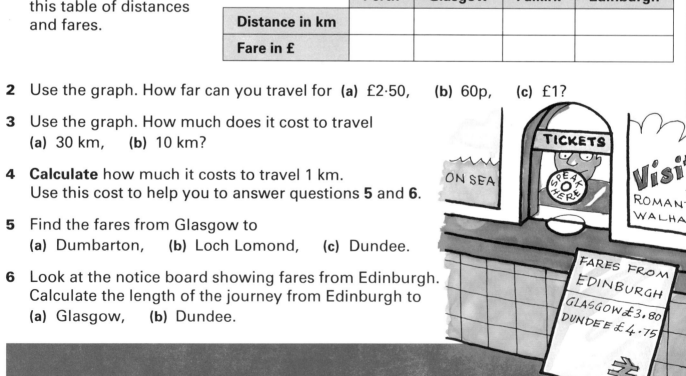

TICKETS

SPEAK O HERE

ON SEA

Visit ROMANT WALHAM

FARES FROM EDINBURGH
GLASGOW £3·80
DUNDEE £4·75

Best buys

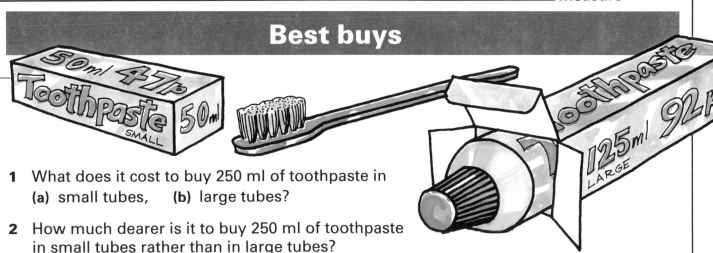

1 What does it cost to buy 250 ml of toothpaste in
(a) small tubes, (b) large tubes?

2 How much dearer is it to buy 250 ml of toothpaste
in small tubes rather than in large tubes?

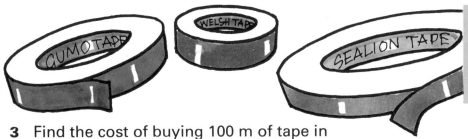

Tape is sold in rolls.

A 50 m roll costs £1·45
A 25 m roll costs 78p
A 10 m roll costs 41p

3 Find the cost of buying 100 m of tape in
(a) 50 m rolls, (b) 25 m rolls, (c) 10 m rolls.

4 How much cheaper is it to buy 100 m of tape in 50 m rolls
rather than in 10 m rolls?

Peanuts are sold in packs.

A 50 g pack costs 23p
A 100 g pack costs 38p
A 300 g pack costs 96p
A 500 g pack costs £1·40

5 How much do you pay for each 50 g of peanuts bought in
(a) a 100 g pack, (b) a 300 g pack, (c) a 500 g pack?

6 How much do you save when you buy 200 g of peanuts
in 100 g packs rather than in 50 g packs?

7 (a) What is the cheapest way to buy 250 g of peanuts
in 100 g and 50 g packs? What does this cost?
(b) Why might it be better to buy a 300 g pack?

8 At school camp 1½ kg of cereal are used each morning.
Find the cost of 1½ kg of cereal bought in
(a) 500 g, (b) 250 g, (c) 750 g packets.

9 The cook wants to buy **as much cereal
as she can** for £5.
(a) Which packets should she buy?
(b) How much money will she have left?

Perimeter of triangles

These equilateral triangles are drawn on centimetre triangular paper.

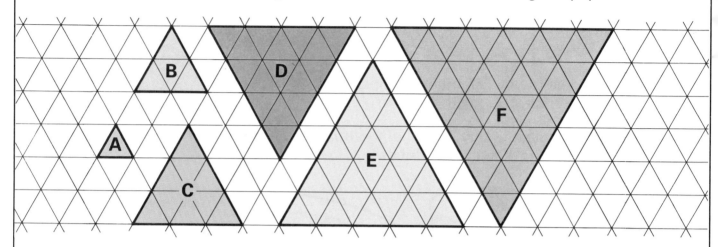

1 Copy and complete this table to show the edge length and perimeter of each triangle.

Triangle	A	B	C	D	E	F
Edge length (cm)						
Perimeter (cm)						

2 (a) Use squared paper and draw axes as shown.
   (b) Mark a cross for each pair of values in your table.
   (c) Put your ruler along the crosses. What do you notice?
   (d) Join the crosses with a straight line.

Use your graph to answer questions 3 to 5.

3 Find the perimeters of equilateral triangles whose edge lengths are
   (a) $2\frac{1}{2}$ cm,   (b) $4\frac{1}{2}$ cm,   (c) $6\frac{1}{2}$ cm.

4 Find the edge lengths of equilateral triangles whose perimeters are
   (a) $4\frac{1}{2}$ cm,   (b) $10\frac{1}{2}$ cm,   (c) $16\frac{1}{2}$ cm.

5 Which word completes this sentence? 'The perimeter of an equilateral triangle is always _____ times the edge length.'

Perimeter of triangles

(graph: Perimeter in cm on vertical axis from 0 to 20; Edge length in cm on horizontal axis from 0 to 6)

6 What is the perimeter of an equilateral triangle whose **edge length** is
   (a) 20 cm,   (b) 100 cm,   (c) 1·5 m,   (d) 2·45 m,   (e) 1·05 m?

7 What is the edge length of an equilateral triangle whose **perimeter** is
   (a) 51 cm,   (b) 96 cm,   (c) 1·5 m,   (d) 2·4 m,   (e) 1·05 m?

Ask your teacher if you should do Measure Cards 42, 44, 46, 48, 50.

Shapes

W

1 Open your **Workbook** at **Page 26**.
From the list below, choose the best name for each shape on that page.
Write that name **on the shape**.

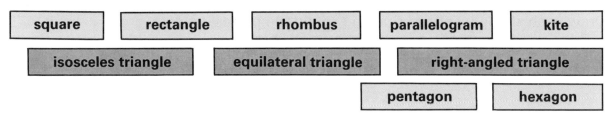

| square | rectangle | rhombus | parallelogram | kite |

| isosceles triangle | equilateral triangle | right-angled triangle |

| pentagon | hexagon |

2 For each shape,
  (a) draw coloured lines to show equal sides,   **(b)** mark any right angles.

3 Cut out all the shapes **A** to **J**.
Draw their lines of symmetry with dotted lines.
You may need to fold the shapes to find these lines.

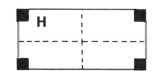

4 Each of these two shapes has all its **sides equal in length**.
Which other shape has all its sides equal?

5 Each of these two shapes has only **1 line of symmetry**.
Which other shape has only 1 line of symmetry?

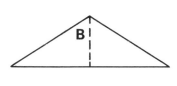
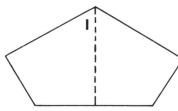

6 Work as a group. Find and name each mystery shape.

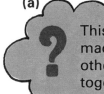
(a) This triangle is made by fitting the other two triangles together.

(b) This shape is half of the pentagon.

(c) This shape has a perimeter of 24 centimetres.

7 Stick all the shapes **A** to **J** in your jotter.

You will use shapes A to J again for Textbook Page 117, question 1.

Making shapes

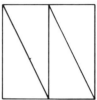

W **1** Stick the four triangles from the top of **Workbook Page 26** on to card.
Cut out the triangles.

2 Fit all **four** triangles together to make each shape below.
Draw each shape by **either** drawing round the pieces,
  or making a small sketch to show
  how the pieces fit together.

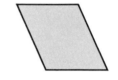

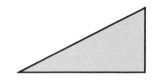

(a) a square   **(b)** a rectangle   **(c)** a parallelogram   **(d)** a right-angled triangle

3 Fit all **four** triangles together to make each shape below. **You will have to
turn over some of the triangles**. Draw each shape below and name it.

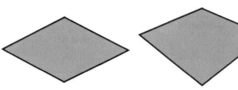

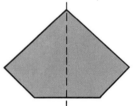

(a) a rhombus   **(b)** a kite   **(c)** a pentagon with
  1 line of symmetry   **(d)** a different pentagon
  with 1 line of symmetry

4 On squared paper draw **four** shapes like this one.
Stick them on to card and cut them out.

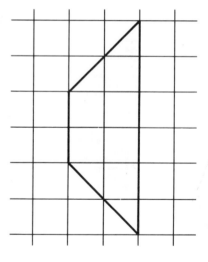

5 Use **two** of your cardboard shapes to make and
then draw each of these:
(a) a hexagon,   **(b)** a parallelogram.

6 Use all **four** shapes to make and then draw each
of these:
(a) a parallelogram,
(b) a square with a square hole in the middle.

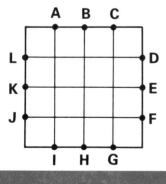

7 Use squared paper.
What shapes do you get if you join each of the
following sets of dots with straight lines?
(a) B → E → K → B   **(b)** A → F → G → L → A
(c) G → E → C → K → G   **(d)** D → H → J → B → D

8 **(a)** List 4 dots you can join to make a square.
(b) Find another set of 4 dots which make a square.

Parallel lines

Railway lines are **parallel**. The rungs of a ladder are **parallel**.
The opposite edges of a window are **parallel**.

These are sets of parallel lines.
We can draw an arrow on each
to show they are parallel.

1 Talk to your teacher about the parallel lines you can see in the drawing above.

2 You can draw along both edges of a
ruler to make parallel lines.

Use your ruler in this way to draw parallel lines and make

(a) a tiling of squares   **(b)** a tiling of rhombuses   **(c)** a design

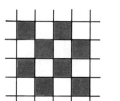   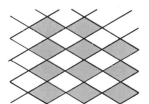

3 Draw a triangle of about this size on plain paper. ──────────────▶

Use your ruler to draw lines parallel to
each side of the triangle like this:

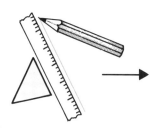 → 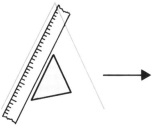 →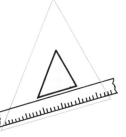

You have drawn an **enlargement** of your triangle.

4 Repeat question **3** starting with a pentagon.

5 **(a)** Draw a triangle which fills a page of your jotter. Use your
ruler to draw parallel lines so that this time you make a
reduction of your triangle.
(b) Do this again starting with a four-sided shape.

Parallel lines

This parallelogram has two pairs of parallel sides.
Each pair is marked with coloured arrows.

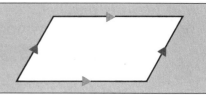

1 Find the shapes you stuck in your jotter when
you did **Textbook Page 114**. Draw coloured arrows
to show any pairs of parallel sides they have.

2 Draw two axes like these on squared paper. Mark
each pair of points. Join them with a straight line.
Line **A** is shown.

Line	Points to join
A	(1,2) to (4,5)
B	(3,2) to (7,1)
C	(13,5) to (9,1)
D	(8,2) to (4,4)
E	(13,1) to (15,3)
F	(6,5) to (12,2)

(a) Which lines are parallel to line **A**?

(b) Which lines are parallel to each other but **not** parallel to line **A**?

3 (a) Draw another two axes on squared paper like the ones in question **2**.

   (b) Mark each set of points. Join the points to make a shape.

   Shape **A**: (2,0) (4,3) (2,6) (0,3)
   Shape **B**: (5,3) (5,1) (7,0) (9,0) (9,3)
   Shape **C**: (9,4) (9,6) (15,2) (15,0)

   (c) Mark pairs of parallel lines with coloured arrows.

4 This line on squared paper goes **along 4 boxes**.
                        and **up 2 boxes**.

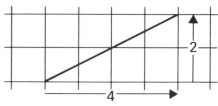

On squared paper, draw **two different lines**
which go along 4 boxes and up 2 boxes. What do you notice about the lines?

**Ask your teacher if you should do Workbook Page 45 and
Shape Cards 62, 64, 66, 68, 70.**

Published by
Heinemann Educational Books Ltd
Halley Court, Jordan Hill, Oxford OX2 8EJ

OXFORD LONDON EDINBURGH MADRID
ATHENS BOLOGNA MELBOURNE SYDNEY
AUCKLAND IBADAN NAIROBI GABORONE
HARARE KINGSTON PORTSMOUTH (NH) SINGAPORE

ISBN 0 435 02829 4
© Scottish Primary Mathematics Group 1987
First published 1987
91 92 93 94 95 10 9 8 7 6 5 4

Designed and typeset by Oxprint Ltd., Oxford
Originated by Jarrold Printing, Norwich
Produced by Mandarin Offset
Printed and bound in Hong Kong